Understanding Criminal Justice
A critical introduction

**Azrini Wahidin
and Nicola Carr**

 Routledge
Taylor & Francis Group

LONDON AND NEW YORK

First published 2013
by Routledge
2 Park Square, Milton Park, Abingdon, Oxon, OX14 4RN

Simultaneously published in the USA and Canada
by Routledge
711 Third Avenue, New York, NY 10017

Routledge is an imprint of the Taylor & Francis Group, an informa business

British Library Cataloguing in Publication Data
A catalogue record for this book is available from the British Library

Library of Congress Cataloging-in-Publication Data
Wahidin, Azrini, 1972–
 Understanding criminal justice: a critical introduction/Azrini Wahidin
and Nicola Carr.
  p. cm.
1. Criminal justice, Administration of–Great Britain–Case studies.
I. Carr, Nicola. II. Title.
HV9960.G7W34 2012
364.941–dc23   2012025646

ISBN: 978–0–415–67021–0 (hbk)
ISBN: 978–0–415–67022–7 (pbk)
ISBN: 978–0–203–08352–9 (ebk)

Typeset in Times New Roman by
Swales & Willis Ltd, Exeter, Devon

MIX
Paper from
responsible sources
FSC® C004839
www.fsc.org

Printed and bound in Great Britain by
TJ International Ltd, Padstow, Cornwall

Understanding Criminal Justice

Few subjects provoke as much public fascination and political concern as crime, criminality, criminology, and criminal justice policy and practice. *Understanding Criminal Justice* seeks to provide students with a critical introduction to the range of theoretical, policy and operational issues faced by the criminal justice system in England, Wales, Scotland and Northern Ireland at the beginning of the twenty-first century.

It anticipates little or no prior knowledge of criminal justice, and seeks to provide an introduction to the area. This critical textbook provides both a thorough overview of the procedures central to the workings of the criminal justice system and a distillation of the topical debates that surround it. It outlines the political and historical context, detailing key procedures and challenging students to engage with current debates. Containing chapters on policing, prosecution, community justice and alternative modes of justice, this text provides a comprehensive coverage of the key topics included within under-graduate criminology programmes at an introductory level.

Written in a lively and accessible style, this book will also be of interest to general readers and practitioners in the criminal justice system.

Azrini Wahidin is a Reader in Criminology and Criminal Justice in the School of Sociology, Social Policy and Social Work, Queen's University Belfast, where she teaches criminology and criminal justice. She has written extensively in the field of older offenders in the criminal justice system and women in prison. Her books include: *Older Women in the Criminal Justice System: Running Out of Time* (Jessica Kingsley, 2004), *Foucault and Ageing* (Nova Press, 2005), *Understanding Prison Staff* (Willan, 2007) and *Ageing, Crime and Society* (Willan, 2006). Her current research interests include the resettlement needs of young offenders and the experiences of Republican political prisoners.

Nicola Carr is a lecturer in the School of Sociology, Social Policy and Social Work, Queen's University Belfast, where she teaches social work law and practice in the criminal justice system. She is a qualified probation officer and has worked with both adults and young people in this context. Her research interests include community sentences, crime and criminal justice in the media, and narrative approaches in the study of offending behaviour.

Contents

Illustrations

Figures

Tables

Boxes

Acknowledgements

In writing a book such as this special thanks go to Nicola Hartley, Tom Sutton and Jules Willan for their support throughout this project. Considerable thanks are also due to the anonymous referees for their invaluable suggestions, which have enriched the final product.

We are grateful to the following for permission to reproduce copyright material: Chapter 1, Figure 1.1, *Hazards* magazine, permission granted by Jawad Qasrawi; Chapter 4, Figure 4.1, UK court structure, permission granted by the UK Supreme Court; Chapter 5, Figure 5.3, offender management map, permission granted by National Offender Management Service (NOMS); Chapter 6, Table 6.2, countries with the most prisoners, permission granted by Helen Fair, The International Centre for Prison Studies; Chapter 7, Figure 7.3, Zahid Mubarek photo, permission granted by Imtiaz Amin, Zahid Mubarek Trust; Chapter 8: Restorative justice case study, permission for use granted by Ray and Vi Donovan (www.chrisdonavantrust.org) and Chris Igoe: Restorative Justice Council.

1   What is crime?

Key issues

- How do we define crime?
- Is something criminal because a legal sanction against it exists?
- How do we count crime?

Introduction

What is crime? This is not an easy question to answer because of the number of different meanings associated with the word crime: crime is a social construction and thus is historically and culturally specific, and embedded in the morality and social norms of that particular society (Bottomley, 1979). We all presume we know what crime is based on commonsense understandings and our own personal experiences; the influence and role of the mass media on defining crime, the role of politicians in shaping understandings of crime and its effects on our everyday lives. For many the concept of crime is linked to our stereotypes of 'criminals' as dangerous others. However, many crimes take place in the home by people we know. We are more likely to be physically and sexually assaulted by family members than strangers (Davies *et al.*, 2007), and we can be harmed by environmental pollution and unsafe working environments (Tombs & Williams, 2008). A study of 'crimes of everyday life' (Karstedt & Farrall, 2006) found that those who saw themselves as 'respectable' and 'law abiding' citizens didn't consider that failing to pay TV licence fees, making false insurance claims or avoiding paying taxes were crimes. Although all of the above are crimes, which activities are perceived as 'normal' or 'deviant' makes defining crime very difficult.

In deconstructing crime, this chapter will show that the concept of crime is diverse and historically relative, and what constitutes crime and how we define

Figure 1.1 Cameron

Source: © Mary Schrider/*Hazards* magazine: www.hazards.org

crime is a contested area. It raises the question as to who has the power to define crime (Chambliss, 1976; Quinney, 1970). Why is it that certain acts get defined as criminal while others do not? Thus, the answer to the question 'what is crime?' depends on the theoretical position taken by those defining crime, which in turn determines the kinds of questions we ask, the nature of the research we conduct and the type of answers that we expect to receive; these in turn produce different kinds of responses to crime. The more thought we give to this question, the more complex defining crime becomes.

The aim of this chapter is thus to explore the meaning of crime and to illustrate how the definitions and meaning of crime are complex and controversial. It is only by looking at the three key approaches to the definitions of crime that we can begin to critically analyse the impact that different perspectives have on the study of crime, understanding crime and researching crime. Crime is not a static category but changes over time and is culturally relative. History is full of examples of individuals, ranging from Aristotle to the suffragette Emmeline Pankhurst to Nelson Mandela, who at one point in history were labelled as criminals and imprisoned but now are considered to be heroes.

Let us consider how changes in society bring about new 'crimes'. For example, the large number of offences connected with vehicles did not exist one hundred years ago, drug offences were not counted until the last thirty years, and cybercrime and computer fraud were virtually non-existent thirty years ago.

In 1981 the most commonly experienced crime was theft of milk bottles from outside a house. Reflecting changing patterns of consumption, this crime had mostly disappeared, and in 2006 vandalism was the most commonly experienced crime (Jansson, 2007).

In the past homosexuality was illegal, and Oscar Wilde (the famous Irish playwright) was convicted in 1895 for 'gross indecency' with another male and sentenced to two years' hard labour, which he served at HMP Wandsworth and Reading gaol.

The *Sexual Offences Act, 1967* (applicable to England and Wales) amended the *Criminal Law Act, 1885* and decriminalised homosexual acts committed in private between two consenting males over the age of 21. However, similar legislation was not passed in Scotland and Northern Ireland until 1980 and 1982 respectively.[1] It is worth noting that similar legislation criminalising consensual sexual acts between adult females has never existed in the United Kingdom, reputedly because legislators did not want to draw women's attention to the fact that such activities occurred.

Cannabis, a drug widely used by doctors (and, allegedly, by Queen Victoria) during the nineteenth century, was available on prescription until 1971. The drug Tetrahydrocannabinol, otherwise known as THC, is a cannabis-based drug used by doctors in Britain as part of treatment for AIDS and cancer patients. In April 2000, an Independent Inquiry established by the Police Foundation concluded that the possession of cannabis should be decriminalised (Runciman, 2000). Following a recommendation in 2002 from the Advisory Council on the Misuse of Drugs, the drug's legal status was downgraded from Class B to Class C, which led to a reduction in the maximum penalty for possession. But by 2009 the Government had reclassified the drug back to Class B (see Box 1.1 and Table 1.1).

Box 1.1   Drug classifications and criminal law

The drug classification system across the legal jurisdictions of the United Kingdom divides drugs into three categories: A, B and C. Class A drugs are those considered to cause most harm. Although *the* question of harm to whom is one that is debated, for example, Professor David Nutt (a former adviser to the Government who was dismissed because of disagreements with the government over its classifications of harm), and colleagues argue:

> Harmful drugs are regulated according to classification systems that purport to relate to the harms and risks of each drug. However, the methodology and processes underlying classification systems are

generally neither specified nor transparent, which reduces confidence in their accuracy and undermines health education messages.

(Nutt *et al.*, 2007: 1047)

The *Misuse of Drugs Act* (1971) states that it is an offence to:

- possess a controlled substance unlawfully
- possess a controlled substance with intent to supply it
- supply or offer to supply a controlled drug (even if it is given away for free)
- allow a house, flat or office to be used by people taking drugs.

The maximum penalties for possession and dealing (a more serious offence) are most severe for Class A drugs (e.g. heroin and crack cocaine) and least severe for Class C drugs (see Table 1.1 for current classifications as designated under the *Misuse of Drugs Act, 1971*).

Table 1.1 Drug classification

		Possession	*Dealing*
Class A	Ecstasy, LSD, Heroin, Cocaine, Crack, Magic Mushrooms, Amphetamines (if prepared for injection).	Up to seven years in prison or an unlimited fine or both.	Up to life in prison or an unlimited fine or both.
Class B	Amphetamines, Cannabis, Methylphenidate (Ritalin), Pholcodine.	Up to five years in prison or an unlimited fine or both.	Up to 14 years in prison or an unlimited fine or both.
Class C	Tranquillisers, some painkillers, Gamma hydroxybutyrate (GHB), Ketamine.	Up to two years in prison or an unlimited fine or both.	Up to 14 years in prison or an unlimited fine or both.

These examples show that criminal laws are not immutable and can be applied varyingly. Criminal law changes over time, which is a reflection of the changing morality and values of society and indeed different political perspectives. Crime therefore is not given but is the consequence of a process, which involves a victim, the perpetrator, the police, lawyers, changing public and political ideology and others who are involved in establishing what constitutes a crime. Owing to the transitory nature of criminal law, it has been argued that a better way should be sought to distinguish between 'acceptable' and 'unacceptable' behaviour within society. However, this has proved to be an easier question to pose than to answer.

Definitions of crime

Crime may appear at first glance easy to define in terms of the infringement of legal codes and thus punishable by the state through the criminal justice process. But how are some actions (or omissions) deemed to be crimes and others not? To begin to answer this question it is useful to look at the different ways we can explore definitions of 'crime' (see Figure 1.2).

Crime can be defined in a variety of ways, and in contemporary criminology a number of definitional perspectives have been adopted that include crime as a legal definition or more broadly as a social construction – in other words, a product of categorisations and classifications (we have already illustrated some of this debate in relation to the classification of illegal drugs). Crime has also been defined as a characteristic of human behaviour, and there is a long lineage within criminology of attempting to classify people according to purportedly criminal characteristics (Hollin, 2007). Broadly speaking, such perspectives adopt psychological or in some cases biological approaches towards understanding crime.

In something of a response to the colonisation of crime under the ambit of criminology, social theorists have also explored crime under the concept of 'harm' (Hillyard *et al.*, 2004). In the following section we explore crime as a legal and social construct, and we examine the usefulness of the concept of 'harm' in opening up our understanding of crime. Our intention here is not to explain fully each type of definition of crime, nor to evaluate the explanatory

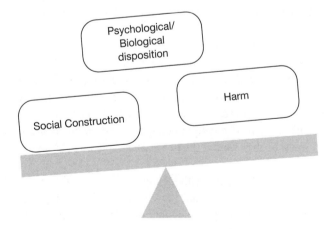

Figure 1.2 Different approaches to understanding crime

merits or usefulness of each definition. Rather we wish to alert the reader to the fact that there are important differences in how people conceive of crime.

Defining crime: a legalistic definition

A formal legal definition specifies that crime is an act or omission proscribed by the criminal law and is subject to state sanction in the form of a specific penalty, and the criminal is the agent who carries out the action. Michael and Adler (1933: 22) provide the following definition: 'the most precise and least ambiguous definition of crime is that which defines it as behaviour which is prohibited by criminal code'. Although the term is rather more difficult to define, Davies *et al.* (2005: 37) offer the following definition of a 'criminal': 'a person whose behaviour is in breach of legally prescribed rules which renders that person liable to criminal proceedings'. This legal classification does not explain why certain conduct is deemed as criminal, it merely helps identify it. This definition as an initial point of discussion is useful in that it highlights three factors: behaviour, breach of rules and the enforcement of punishment.

In terms of behaviour, criminal law is concerned with the regulation of behaviour and not the causes of criminal behaviour. The rules that determine whether behaviour is criminal are found in legislation introduced by Acts of Parliament. In the United Kingdom criminal law can be enacted in Westminster and in the regional assemblies of Northern Ireland and Scotland (the contours of the different criminal jurisdictions are discussed further in the next chapter). Statute law (legislation) is often used to decriminalise old offences, create new offences, redefine or modify offences that already exist or consolidate old pieces of legislation on the same topic. These form the starting point for understanding crime as they provide the legal definition of criminal acts.

The criminal law and the types of punishment are used against a range of behaviours from murder to parking on double yellow lines. Most people consider acts such as murder or rape to be wrong (or evil) in themselves. This is encapsulated in the Latin phrase: *malum in se* (wrong in themselves) (Lacey, 2007). Such acts are also prohibited by criminal law. Other acts are defined as criminal by virtue of the fact that they are prohibited; this is referred to as *malum prohibitum* (Lacey *et al.*, 2010). The police typically enforce criminal laws. A range of other agencies are involved in what is collectively known as the 'criminal justice system' in the prosecution, adjudication and enforcement of sentences (the functioning of the criminal justice system is dealt with in the next chapter).

However, laws are social products, and without law defining a particular act as criminal there can be no crime. Sutherland (1945), regarded by many as a founding figure in American criminology, noted that in order for behaviour to be defined as criminal it required two main elements:

1. A legal description of the act as socially injurious
2. Legal provision of a penalty for such an act.

However, in his discussion of what he termed 'white collar crime' – that is, crimes committed by a person in a position of status for financial gain, Sutherland (1945) noted that the law tended to be differentially applied.[2] Firstly, offences in this category (e.g. tax evasion, copyright infringement) were usually differently categorised and, secondly, they were processed in a different manner and tended not to attract the full stigma of criminal sanction. He argued that such distinctions were not sustainable and that definitions of crime and criminality should take full account of the nature of the social injury/harm caused. Therefore, for Sutherland, an adequate definition of crime should be based on an expanded definition of harm that includes 'social injury'. Similarly, Quinney (1977) wanted to expand the definition of crime to include not only the legal harms resulting from economic domination in a capitalist society, but also the crimes of government and of their agencies of social control. This led the American sociologist Tappan (1947) to define crime as:

> . . . an intentional act in violation of the criminal law . . . committed without defence or excuse, and penalised by the state as a felony or misdemeanour (more or less serious criminal acts). In studying the offender there can be no presumption that . . . persons are criminals unless they also be held guilty beyond a reasonable doubt of a particular offence.
>
> (Tappan, 1947: 100)

Tappan (1947) disagreed with expanding the legal definition, arguing that without adhering strictly to law, it would render the concept of crime as open-ended and devoid of meaning.

However, a major criticism of the legalistic approach is that it supports those in power who are able to influence the making of laws and the imposition of criminal definitions on lawbreakers. Secondly, legalistic definitions of crime fail to include the social, ethical and individual significance of forms of behaviour. Thirdly, categories of 'crime' given by the criminal justice system fail to reflect the experiences of victims in general, thus providing a rationale for abandoning the notion of 'crime' as a tool in the conceptual framework of criminology because crime has no ontological reality. As Zedner (2004) observes, 'crime' may be viewed both as a criminal and civil wrong simultaneously, and thus the legal classification doesn't help tell us to understand why or how certain conduct is defined as criminal, it merely helps define it. Zedner (2004: 61) further elaborates: 'to think about crime, as some criminal law textbooks still do, as comprising discrete autonomous legal categories remote from the social world, is to engage in an absorbing but esoteric intellectual activity'.

Much of what criminologists do uses categories derived from the criminal law and, moreover, uses statistics taken from the operation of criminal justice agencies enforcing or administering the criminal justice law. Does this mean that there is nothing common to all those things that are the objects of our study as criminologists other than are defined as 'criminal'? Can we limit our attention solely to those things that might lead to a conviction in a criminal court? Or do we expand the definition of crime to include social harm? This will be discussed later on in the chapter.

In the next section we turn our attention to the sociological definition of crime.

Sociological definition: consensus

Traditional explanations of crime assume that society is based on a consensus of values and that the criminal law reflects this. Moreover, consensus theorists circumvent the problem of variations in law by tying the definition of crime to social morality. The term 'consensus' refers to the extent of social agreement about whether victims have been harmed. Official societal response refers to the existence of criminal laws specifying under what conditions (such as intent and knowledge of the consequences) that an act resulting in harm can be called crime, and the enforcement of such laws against those committing acts that harm.

The French sociologist Emile Durkheim argued that crime serves to establish and clarify the moral boundaries of society. Thus emerged what became known as the *moral* or *consensus* position on crime, which holds that crimes are acts that shock the common or collective morality – the conscience collective – producing moral outrage among people. Durkheim stated that, 'an act is criminal when it offends the strong, well-defined states of the collective consciousness' (1984 [1893]: 39). By identifying those behaviours deemed unacceptable, society reaffirms and refines what is acceptable. Specifically, crime was a term used, 'to designate any act, which, regardless of degree, provokes against the perpetrator the characteristic reaction known as punishment' (1984 [1893]: 31). As a result, the basic definition of crime became behaviour defined and sanctioned by criminal law. Thus there is no crime without law, and law is based on the 'injury' or 'harm done'.

In the late 1960s and early 1970s, radical and critical criminologists further challenged conceptions of crime and criminality. They argued that the problem of crime was indeed tied to the law, but only insofar as those who made the law criminalised the harmful behaviour of some, but not others, notably the powerful. In some respects this echoed some of Sutherland's (1945) earlier interrogation of the concept of 'white collar crime'. We can see therefore that criminalisation is one of the many ways of constructing social reality. In fact the Dutch abolitionist lawyer Louk Hulsman noted that categories of 'crime' are created by the criminal justice system itself and in order to study the topic critically, he argued:

> This makes it necessary to abandon the notion of 'crime' as a tool in the conceptual framework of criminology. Crime has no ontological reality. Crime is not the object by the product of criminal policy. Criminalization is one of the many ways of constructing social reality.
>
> (Hulsman, 1986: 71)

This then begs the question, why is it that some acts get defined as criminal while others do not? For example, Henry and Milovanovic (1996: 104) state that: 'crimes are nothing less than moments in the expression of power such that those who are subjected to these expressions are denied their own contribution to the encounter and often to future encounters'. They argue that crime 'is the power to deny others . . . in which those subject to the power of another, suffer the pain of being denied their own humanity, the power to make a difference'. Thus, if we are to explain and understand the nature of crime then we must first explain the social forces that cause some acts to be defined criminal while other acts are not.

Crime as social harm

Other theorists have argued that we should replace 'crime' as an organising concept and consider instead the concept of *social harm* and injury tied to the notion of human rights. Hillyard *et al.* (2004) use the term *Zemiology*, which derives from the Greek word *Zemia*, meaning harm – so Zemiology is the study of harm and includes all types of harms people experience from the cradle to the grave. Harms according to this perspective have been divided into three main types:

1. Physical harms – e.g. accidents at work and on the road; domestic violence, criminal assaults, and pollution;
2. Financial harms – e.g. mis-selling of mortgages or other financial rip-offs; and
3. Emotional harms.

Some of the harmful events may be criminal but, unlike criminology, which takes a State-defined position as its starting point, this perspective adopts a much wider approach and considers all harms that people experience. This approach says that crime occurs whenever a human right has been violated, both criminal offences (e.g. assault) and civil offences (e.g. negligence), in that each type of action brings with it some type of harm and thus should attract some type of penalty regardless of the legality or otherwise of the action. Thus harms of repression have also been described as crimes against human dignity: 'acts and conditions that obstruct the spontaneous unfolding of human potential' (Tifft, 1995: 9). Such a conception also expands the definition of crime to include oppressive practices such as racism, sexism and class-based exploitation.

Crime statistics and recording of crime

Whatever perspective we choose to adopt in order to understand the meaning and definition of 'crime', we cannot ignore the fact that the manner in which crime is officially categorised and recorded contributes to our understanding and construction of the 'problem' of crime. The final section of this chapter highlights a number of key themes in this respect. Some key points are important to note here. Firstly, by no means all crime is recorded. Secondly, particular types of crime are under-recorded for a range of reasons, which are explored. Thirdly, the actual processing of cases through the criminal justice system (discussed more fully in the next chapter) is affected by *attrition*.

Most of our information on crime comes from 'official' sources, such as police and court records. A crime is officially recorded when it is reported to or detected by the police. However, as numerous studies reveal, official data on crime obtained from police records represents only a small proportion of all crime committed (Maguire, 2007). This is demonstrated by the fact that victim surveys, which ask people to anonymously record if they have been a victim of crime, routinely record much higher rates of crime than the official statistics of criminal justice agencies reveal. Self-reported data (i.e. surveys that ask people to anonymously record offences they have committed) also reveals a much higher rate of crime than is officially recorded. In other words, while official crime data may be able to provide us with an indication of broad trends, it only ever give us a partial picture of the 'true' crime rate if such a thing can be said to exist (Maguire, 2007) – see Box 1.2.

Box 1.2   The Crime Survey for England and Wales

The Crime Survey for England and Wales (formerly known as the British Crime Survey) is a face-to-face victimisation survey in which a sample of people resident in England and Wales are asked questions about their experiences of crime and victimisation. Separate crime victim surveys are conducted in Scotland (Scottish Crime and Justice Survey) and Northern Ireland (Northern Ireland Crime Victims Survey). International crime victim surveys that are conducted under the auspices of the United Nations Interregional Crime and Justice Institute (UNICRI) are also

---

available for a range of countries. The International Crime Victim Survey (ICVS) covers around 37,000 respondents in 18 different countries, and includes data on England, Wales, Northern Ireland and Scotland.

The Crime Survey for England and Wales annually includes about 47,000 participants. This has increased from the first survey sample in 1982, which included 11,000 participants. The survey asks participants about their experiences of crime in the 12 months prior to interview. Participants are also asked about their attitudes to crime, the role of various criminal justice agencies and their perception of crime and anti-social behaviour.

Traditionally the survey has just included respondents over the age of 16, leading to a criticism that crime against children and young people was under-represented. However, since 2009 interviews have been carried out with young people aged 10–15. The Crime Survey for England and Wales has been restricted to people in private residential accommodation, therefore it does not include people living in institutions or communal establishments or people living on the streets. Other limitations include the fact that the survey does not include crimes that are victimless and crimes such as murders where the victim cannot be interviewed. The latter limitation is not as significant, however, as murder tends to be a crime that is highly reported to the police.

The Crime Survey for England and Wales provides a better reflection of overall crime than police statistics because it includes crimes that have not been reported to the police. Illustrating this point, the first British Crime Survey conducted in 1982 (reporting on crime in 1981) estimated that there were 11 million crimes in England and Wales, but there were less than three million crimes recorded by the police (Jansson, 2007).

Reasons for under-reporting of crime

It is evident that only a proportion of crimes are reported to or detected by the police. There are a number of reasons why crime may be unreported and unrecorded. A crime may be unreported because it is a so-called 'victimless' offence, for example, someone selling drugs to another person who wants to purchase them. Other crimes may be unreported because victims may not know where to seek help or may fear retribution from the perpetrator – domestic violence and child sexual abuse are examples. Sexual crimes are generally under-reported, and research with people who have experienced such crimes identifies that the fear of being disbelieved and a concern that the criminal process itself will be further traumatising are barriers to reporting (Fergusson *et al*., 2000; Walsh *et al*., 2008).

Another widely under-reported category of crime is crimes based on hate. *Hate crimes* are defined as crimes that are based on a hostility, prejudice or hatred of someone or some group because of some aspect of their identity such as:

- Disability
- Gender identity
- Race, ethnicity or nationality
- Political affiliation
- Religion or belief
- Sexual orientation.

Examples of hate crimes include verbal harassment, graffiti, physical attacks and murder. In England and Wales the *Crime and Disorder Act, 1998* made hate towards a victim based on the above attributes an aggravating factor for specified offences. In other words, where this was proven a court could sentence the perpetrator more severely than would otherwise be the case. The introduction of this legislation into England and Wales was in part influenced by the aftermath of the Stephen Lawrence case (discussed in Chapter 3).

The English and Welsh legislation had been pre-dated by law introduced to Northern Ireland in 1987 *(Public Order (Northern Ireland) Order, 1987)*, which prohibited behaviour based on hatred and the intention to 'arouse fear'. This legislation was introduced in the context of the 30-year civil and political conflict in Northern Ireland known as the *Troubles,* where sectarian-based violence had claimed many lives and injured many more. Scotland introduced legislation relating to incitement to racial hatred in 1986, and more recently it has introduced legislation that provides that offences based on 'malice and ill will' towards an individual based on their sexual orientation, transgender identity or disability are aggravating factors to be considered in sentencing.[3]

A further factor in discrepancies in recorded crime data and a final outcome such as a conviction in court relate to what is called *attrition.* This means that even when crimes are reported they may not proceed to prosecution, or if prosecuted there may not be a 'successful' outcome from the point of view of the victim. As cases progress through the criminal justice system there are various points of 'attrition'. For example, when the police pass the case file of a crime to the prosecution service, this service must decide if the case meets certain criteria. These criteria include whether the case meets evidential requirements, that is, is the evidence of a standard that could result in a successful prosecution? It must also be decided if prosecution of the offence is in the 'public interest'. Cases that do proceed to court may collapse for a number of reasons, for example, if the correct legal process is not followed (these issues are discussed more fully in the next chapter). There are also cases where the criminal process is abused, leading to wrongful convictions – this is referred to as a 'miscarriage of justice' and is discussed further in Chapter 3.

Conclusion

In this chapter, we have shown that although the definition of a crime is generally treated as non-problematic, this in fact is far from the case. The chapter has provided an introduction to some of the main perspectives in the approaches to defining crime. Crime and the study of crime occur within a social and political context. Each perspective influences the way we approach the study of crime and deviance and the methods we use. It raises the question around the consequences and implication of accepting one definition over others. It also shows that there is no common element to a crime other than the fact of the prior legal procedure defining an act or omission as a crime. By deconstructing the meaning of crime we can ask the questions: who defines the law, who makes the laws and why are they made? Whose interests are reflected in those laws and how are they enforced? What about cases today where people may actively break the law in the name of social justice? There are unjust systems in the world, and it might well be the case that many legal definitions are built on highly contentious and unjust or unfair propositions.

Perhaps unsurprisingly, then, we see that official crime statistics do not encapsulate the nature and extent of crime. There are a number of suggested reasons for this, including issues of confidence in the criminal justice system (an issue that we turn to in the next chapter). The overall conclusion is that, as McCabe (1983) avers, 'there is no word in the whole lexicon of legal and criminological terms which is so elusive of definition as the word "crime"'. How then, he asks, 'can the discipline that has as its common focus the study of crime ever have a settled focus?' (1983: 49).

Glossary

Attrition – is used in the context of the criminal justice system to refer to criminal cases that do not proceed any further through the system. This can be for a variety of reasons, including insufficient evidence to charge or prosecute someone for the offence or deterioration in evidence because of a delay in bringing the case to court.

Hate crime – is defined by (Perry 2001: 10) as: '. . . acts of violence and intimidation, usually directed towards already stigmatised and marginalised groups. As such, it is a mechanism of power and oppression, intended to reaffirm the precarious hierarchies that characterise a given social order . . .'

Zemiology – involves the study of 'social harms', it is derived from the Greek word 'harm' and is intended as a critique of criminology's narrow focus on harm as confined to legally sanctioned criminal acts.

Case study

Decriminalisation of homosexuality in Northern Ireland

Jeff Dudgeon, a young Northern Irish man, was interrogated by the police about his sexual activities with men in 1975. At this time in Northern Ireland homosexuality was illegal and thus criminalised. This led to a landmark test case, *Dudgeon* v. *The United Kingdom*, which was heard at the European Court of Human Rights (ECHR). It was held that legislation criminalising sexual acts between consenting adult males was in contravention of Article 8 (referring to the right to privacy) of the ECHR.

The case was significant, for a number of reasons. Firstly, it was a successful case before the ECHR on the criminalisation of male homosexuality. Secondly, it was the case that, in 1982, made the law on male homosexuality in Northern Ireland the same as it was in Scotland (since 1980), and in England and Wales (since 1967). As a consequence of the judgment, male homosexual sex was decriminalised in Northern Ireland in October 1982. In comparison, lesbian behaviour has never been criminal anywhere in the United Kingdom.

Male homosexuality remained illegal in the Republic of Ireland until 1993, following the ECHR decision in Norris v Ireland (1988), for which Dudgeon v The United Kingdom was the keystone precedent.

Seminar questions

1. Why do you think the law in respect of male homosexuality has changed in the UK over time?
2. What in your view is the basis for reclassification of cannabis as a Class B drug?
3. Why are some crimes under-reported?

Further information can be obtained from the following websites

Information on the *Crime Survey for England and Wales* (formerly the *British Crime Survey)* is available from the Office for National Statistics website. This contains information on the methodology used for data collection: http://www.ons.gov.uk/ons/taxonomy/index.html?nscl=Crime+in+England+and+Wales

Information on the Northern Ireland crime survey is available from the website of the Northern Ireland Statistics and Research Agency (NISRA): http://www.csu.nisra.gov.uk/survey.asp8.htm

Crime and justice statistics for Scotland are available from the website of the Scottish government. This website contains information on the Scottish Crime and Justice Survey as well as a range of government publications on crime data: http://www.scotland.gov.uk/Topics/Statistics/Browse/Crime-Justice

Further reading

Coleman, R., Sim, J., Tombs, S. & Whyte, D. (2010) *State, Power, Crime.* **London: Sage**
This book provides an overview of some key debates around the categorisation of crime, particularly in relation to structural dimensions including race, gender, class and sexuality.

Nutt, D., King, L.A., Saulsbury, W. & Blakemore, C. (2007) 'Development of a rational scale to assess the harm of drugs of potential misuse', *The Lancet,* **369, 9566: 1047–53**
This article contains a detailed overview of some of the recent debates about the concept of harm and drug classification, and it presents a rationale for adopting a different approach towards the classification of harm.

Sutherland, E. (1945) 'Is "White Collar Crime" crime?', *American Sociological Review,* **10, 2: 132–9**
This paper, written in the first half of the last century, when criminology was an emergent discipline, provides an interesting insight into debates about crime and criminality through Sutherland's interrogation of the concept of 'White Collar Crime'.

References

Bottomley, K. (1979) 'What is crime?' In: *Criminology in Focus: Past Trends and Future Prospects.* Oxford: Martin Robertson, pp. 1–39

Chambliss, W. (1976) 'The State and criminal law'. In: W. Chambliss & M. Mankoff (eds) *Whose Law? What Order? A Conflict Approach to Criminology.* New York: John Wiley

Davies, M., Croall, H. & Tyrer, J. (2005) *Criminal Justice: An Introduction to the Criminal Justice System in England and Wales.* London: Longman

Davies, P., Francis, P. & Greer, C. (2007) *Victims, Crime and Society.* London: Sage

Durkheim, E. (1984 [1893]). *The Division of Labour in Society.* New York: The Free Press

Fergusson, D.M., Horwood, L.J. & Woodward, J.J. (2000) 'The stability of child abuse reports: A longitudinal study of reporting behaviour of young adults', *Psychological Medicine,* 30, 3: 529–44

Henry, S. & Milovanovic, D. (1996) *Constitutive Criminology: Beyond Postmodernism.* London: Sage

Hillyard, P., Pantazis, C., Tombs, S. & Gordon, D. (eds) (2004) *Beyond Criminology: Taking Harm Seriously.* London: Pluto Press

Hollin, C. (2007) 'Criminological psychology'. In: M. Maguire, R. Morgan & R. Reiner (eds) (2007) *The Oxford Handbook of Criminology*, 4th edn. Oxford: Oxford University Press, pp. 43–78

Hulsman, L.H.C. (1986) 'Critical criminology and the concept of crime', *Contemporary Crises*, 10, 1: 63–80

Jansson, K. (2007) *British Crime Survey – Measuring Crime for 25 Years*. London: Home Office

Karstedt, S. & Farrall, S. (2006) 'The moral economy of everyday crime: Markets, consumers and citizens', *British Journal of Criminology*, 46, 6: 1011–36

Lacey, N. (2007) 'Legal constructions of crime'. In: M. Maguire, R. Morgan and R. Reiner (eds) *The Oxford Handbook of Criminology*, 4th edn. Oxford: Oxford University Press, pp. 179–201

Lacey, N., Wells, C. & Quick, O. (2010) *Reconstructing Criminal Law*, 4th edn. Cambridge: Cambridge University Press

McCabe, S. (1983) 'Crime'. In: D. Walsh and A. Poole (eds) *A Dictionary of Criminology*. London: Routledge & Kegan Paul

Maguire, M. (2007) 'Crime data and statistics'. In: M. Maguire, R. Morgan & R. Reiner (eds) *The Oxford Handbook of Criminology*, 4th edn. Oxford: Oxford University Press, pp. 241–90

Michael, J. & Adler, M. (1933) *Crime, Law and Social Science*. New York: Harcourt Brace Jovanovich

Nutt, D., King, L.A., Salusbury, W. & Blakemore, C. (2007) 'Development of a rational scale to assess the harm of drugs of potential misuse', *The Lancet*, 369, 9566: 1047–53

Perry, B. (2001) *In the Name of Hate: Understanding Hate Crimes*. London: Routledge

Quinney, R. (1970) *The Social Reality of Crime*. New York: Little Brown Company

Quinney, R. (1977) *Class, State and Crime: On the Theory and Practice of Criminal Justice*. New York: David McKay Company Inc.

Runciman, R. (2000) *Drugs and the Law: Report of the Independent Inquiry into the Misuse of Drugs Act 1971*. London: Police Foundation

Sutherland, E. (1945) 'Is "White Collar Crime" crime?', *American Sociological Review*, 10, 2: 132–9

Sutherland, E. (1949) *White Collar Crime*. New York: Holt, Rinehart & Winston

Tappan, P. (1947) 'Who is the criminal?', *American Sociological Review*, 12: 97–102

Tifft, L. (1995) 'Social harm definitions of crime', *The Critical Criminologist*, 7, 1: 9–13

Tombs, S. & Williams, B. (2008) 'Corporate crimes and its victims'. In: B. Stout, J. Yeats & B. Williams (eds) *Applied Criminology*. London: Sage, pp. 170–84

Walsh, W.A., Lippert, T., Cross, T.P., Maurice, D.M. & Davison, K.S. (2008) 'How long to prosecute child sexual abuse for a community using a children's advocacy center and two comparison communities?', *Child Maltreatment*, 13, 1: 3–13

Zedner, L. (2004) *Criminal Justice*. Clarendon Law Series. Oxford: Oxford University Press

2　What is the criminal justice system?

Key issues

*   What is the criminal justice system?
*   What are the main agencies that constitute the system?
*   Is criminal justice a 'system'?

Introduction

Discussing the criminal justice system in the United Kingdom presents a unique challenge. The government of the United Kingdom consists of a national parliament in Westminster, and three devolved regional assemblies in Scotland, Wales and Northern Ireland. The regional assemblies have law-making powers and separate governance arrangements for their national criminal justice systems. Scotland, Wales and Northern Ireland, for example, each have a separate minister with responsibility for their national criminal justice system. Thus the specific contours of criminal justice policy and therefore the criminal justice system differ in each of the constituent jurisdictions of the United Kingdom.

The terms used to describe different components of the system can also differ. For example, in England and Wales the state prosecutor, that is, the agency that decides whether to proceed to prosecute a criminal case, is called the *Crown Prosecution Service (CPS)*; in Northern Ireland this agency is called the *Public Prosecution Service (PPS)*; and in Scotland it is called the *Crown Office and Procurator Fiscal Service (COPFS)*. In essence, however, all of these agencies carry out similar functions. Notwithstanding some important differences in the criminal justice system and agencies in the United Kingdom, this chapter sets out to explore some of the key themes in the criminal justice process and system, which are broadly similar across the UK.

Firstly, the chapter discusses what is meant by the criminal justice system and questions the idea of a system as such. The next section focuses on the agencies and examines the types of disposals available. The criminal justice system has a number of aims, central of which is the detection of crime, the apprehension of offenders, ensuring that due process is followed and that a penalty is imposed to reflect the seriousness of the offence committed. This at least is the theory.

The image of justice is portrayed as a woman holding the scales of justice in one hand and the sword of truth in the other, blindfolded to signify the impartiality of justice, which is 'balanced'/'neutral' and equally applied to *all*, irrespective of place, gender, sexual preference, age, ability, ethnicity, 'race', religious or political belief, wealth or status. However, this symbol or abstraction becomes problematic (as this book will demonstrate) when it is applied in the 'real world' of twenty-first-century Britain. The extent to which the criminal justice system is able to deliver 'justice for all' is limited by the broader structural and social inequalities of the society in which the system operates. These inequalities include poverty, poor housing and education, ill-health, unemployment and poor environmental conditions, all of which are associated with the effective denial of full social citizenship.

What is the criminal justice system for?

Before proceeding further we must pose the question: what is the criminal justice system for? Various theorists have debated this topic, and it is evident perhaps that the criminal justice system is one of the ways in which society is governed and the way in which social order is maintained. Laws, which prohibit certain types of behaviour, are the scaffolding on which the criminal justice system is built. Such laws are reflective of societal norms, that is, what a society deems to be acceptable or not. So, for example, there are laws that seek to prohibit causing physical injury to another person (assault) or taking goods without payment (theft). Such behaviour is defined in law as a crime, but, as we have seen from the previous chapter, the question of how crime is defined is open to debate. The law sets out the formal sanctions that will apply if such crimes are committed. For example, the *Sexual Offences Act, 2003* applicable in England and Wales outlines that the offence of rape is punishable by imprisonment for life, indicating the seriousness in which such an offence is viewed.[1]

Alongside the maintenance of social order and the expression of social norms, the criminal justice system (or more accurately its constituent parts) has a range of other functions, some of which ebb and flow over time. For example, we can say that one of the purposes of the criminal justice system is the punishment of offenders. This is manifest in sentences to prison or 'punishment in the community' in the form of community penalties (e.g. probation order) (Brownlee, 1998).

The prevention of crime is another stated aim of the system; consider, for example, the role of the police whose visible presence in public areas is primarily aimed towards preventing crime. Some would argue that prison sentences also have a preventative effect – for one thing, they incapacitate the person imprisoned, therefore preventing further reoffending in the community – but also it is argued that such visible punishment has a deterrent effect, that is, it may result in less crime because people fear the consequences. Such rationales are highly contested, as rates of reoffending among people subject to a prison sentence are relatively high and the prison population in England and Wales has risen significantly in the past twenty years, somewhat negating the argument of a 'deterrent effect' (Morgan & Liebling, 2007).

Rehabilitation is also put forward as an underpinning rationale of the criminal justice system, although this particular aim came under sustained attack, particularly over the latter part of the twentieth century, when the effectiveness of rehabilitative measures was strongly critiqued (Ward & Maruna, 2007).

The fact that the aims and purposes of the criminal justice system can oscillate is reflective of the fact that the 'system' is a conglomeration of a range of separate agencies with different functions – what the police do, for example, is very different from what the prison service does. It is also, however, a product of the fact that the criminal justice system is a highly politicised arena, where political debate and government policies can profoundly influence the nature of practice. The so-called 'law and order' policies of the Conservative government and subsequent Labour governments throughout the 1990s, which vowed to be 'tough on crime', have been linked, for example, to the rise in the prison population in England and Wales in this period (Young & Matthews, 2003). However, in Northern Ireland the transition to a post-conflict society has meant that the overall numbers in prison have declined in the same period as new institutional arrangements have been put in place (Ellison & Mulcahy, 2009). In Scotland some commentators have argued that following devolution there has been an increased politicisation of criminal justice and an erosion of 'welfarist' principles that previously distinguished this system (Croall, 2006).

These examples serve to highlight that the criminal justice system is not devoid of social reference but is embedded in particular spatial, cultural, historical, political, economic and social contexts. This in turn raises the following questions of how a criminal justice system can be defined and described: What does it do? What are its key elements? What is it for? Would it be accurate to describe the criminal justice system as a *system*, and how systematic is criminal justice in the United Kingdom?

These questions are complex, and the following chapters will explore them in detail. Before before doing so, we must first look at how the criminal justice system is organised, what it is for and what are the functions performed by its constituent agencies? Within the criminal justice system the reader will see that there is a complexity and multiplicity of processes, actors and agencies with a shared objective to regulate 'potential, alleged and actual criminal activity within procedural limits [which are] supposed to protect the citizen from wrongful treatment and wrongful conviction' (Sanders & Young, 2000: 10).

How the criminal justice system operates

At a very simplistic level criminal justice is delivered through a series of stages: charge; trial; sentence; appeal; punishment. The criminal justice system is a term encompassing all those institutions that respond officially to the commission of offences – notably, the police, prosecution authorities, the courts and the probation and prison services. These are referred to collectively as the criminal justice system. The overarching objectives of the system, as defined by Sanders and Young (2000: ibid.), is to regulate 'potential, alleged and actual criminal activity within procedural limits that are supposed to protect the citizen from wrongful treatment and wrongful conviction'. In the following section and throughout the succeeding chapters, we will challenge the idea of the criminal justice system being a 'joined-up system' by examining how in practice criminal justice agencies operate to perform their key functions.

As already outlined, there are three distinctive criminal justice systems with separate procedures and agencies in the United Kingdom: England and Wales; Scotland; and Northern Ireland. The Ministry of Justice for England and Wales, the Justice Department in Scotland and the Department of Justice in Northern Ireland are responsible for criminal justice in the three jurisdictions. Some overarching justice policy and functions are implemented at a 'national' (i.e. at whole-UK level) and are coordinated by the Home Office; these include counter-terrorism operations, border controls and the security service (MI5).[2] While these are clearly important areas, here our primary focus is the 'domestic' criminal justice arena. Across the jurisdictions a broadly similar range of processes applies for adults who are accused of a crime. Separate systems and process operate for children and young people, (under the age of 18), and these are fully described in Chapter 7.

The next section details the criminal justice process from the detection or reporting of an offence to the imposition of a penalty. Different agencies are responsible for each stage of the process, and throughout a person, variously described as a suspect, a defendant or an offender (depending on the stage and status of the process), will come under the auspices of the different agencies that comprise the *criminal justice system*.

A joined-up system?

Although we have used the term 'criminal justice system', some might challenge whether it is a system at all. We must now look at what this implies, and ask the question, what is meant by this term? What does it consist of and how does it work? The term 'system' is often used to describe a unit such as a central heating system or a natural phenomenon such as the solar system (Wilson & Ashton, 2001). The word 'system' implies an object with interconnected, interdependent parts, subdivisions and a set of coordinated decision-making bodies. It will become evident throughout this book that many groups working within the criminal justice system are relatively autonomous. Nonetheless, the inaccuracy of the term 'system' should not obscure the practical interdependence of the various bodies.

The assembly of components that constitutes the criminal justice process demonstrates that many criminal justice agencies depend on other criminal justice bodies for their caseload or for their information, and decisions taken by one agency can impinge on those taken by others. Thus, to take a few examples: prosecution services depend almost entirely on the police for the information on which to make their decision. A prosecution service's decisions in turn affect the caseload of the courts, and may constrain the power of courts and of the defendant to determine the mode of trial (this will be explained in Chapter 4).

The criminal justice system impinges directly on victims, suspects and defendants. It affects them in the form of one or more contacts and decisions. For example, a defendant who has been questioned by the police, charged, kept in police custody, remanded by the court, perhaps offered a plea bargain, and then tried in court is already likely to feel 'punished' irrespective of whether a guilty verdict and sentence follow.

Although this assembly of parts are interdependent they also work within their own remit, creating at times a disjuncture between the parts. Some prefer to see criminal justice as a process through which a case or a defendant passes. In this process all stages are governed by a set of discrete rules, are interrelated and affect the eventual outcome (see Uglow, 2002). For the purpose of this book we will refer to the criminal justice process as the criminal justice system.

The main agencies of the criminal justice system

The criminal justice system is made up of a variety of agencies and organisations, each with its own responsibilities and areas of decision-making authority. In the United Kingdom criminal justice agencies such as the police and prisons are funded primarily by central government. The main agencies are as follows, and even this is not a complete list.

Police

The criminal justice process normally starts to operate only when a crime is reported to the police, and, as discussed in the previous chapter, by no means are all crimes reported. In England and Wales the range of powers of the police to carry out searches and to arrest and question suspects in pursuit of their investigations is set out in the *Police and Criminal Evidence Act, 1984 (PACE)* and accompanying codes of practice. Similar rules of police operations apply in Northern Ireland, but there is no equivalent to PACE in Scotland.[3] Police codes of practice outline the statutory powers of the police to 'stop and search', and require that the police officer makes a full record of any such activity. The police powers of arrest and treatment of suspects in custody are also proscribed. For example, Box 2.1 outlines what is said in the PACE Code in respect of arrest.

Box 2.1   Extract from PACE Code of Practice on the Statuory Power of Arrest

The right to liberty is a key principle of the Human Rights Act 1998. The exercise of the power of arrest represents an obvious and significant interference with that right.

1.3 The use of the power must be fully justified and officers exercising the power should consider if the necessary objectives can be met by other, less intrusive means. Arrest must never be used simply because it can be used. Absence of justification for exercising the powers of arrest may lead to challenges should the case proceed to court. When the power of arrest is exercised it is essential that it is exercised in a non-discriminatory and proportionate manner.

A lawful arrest requires two elements:
A person's involvement or suspected involvement or attempted involvement in the commission of a criminal offence;

AND
Reasonable grounds for believing that the person's arrest is necessary.

2.2 Arresting officers are required to inform the person arrested that they have been arrested, even if this fact is obvious, and of the relevant circumstances of the arrest in relation to both elements and to inform the custody officer of these on arrival at the police station...

Extract from PACE Code of Practice
(p. 218 Code G: Statutory Power of Arrest by Police Officers)

If the police believe that there is sufficient evidence they can charge a suspect and decide whether the suspect is to be bailed or remanded in police custody after charge: this is the first stage of the prosecution process. The defendant may be bailed to appear in court or, if there are reasonable grounds for believing that detention is necessary for certain purposes, the police may keep the defendant in custody until the first court appearance.

There are 43 regional police forces in England and Wales each under the direction of a chief constable, except for the Metropolitan Police and the City of London Police, who have commissioners. Under new government proposals, from November 2012 each police force in England and Wales will have a publicly elected 'Police and Crime Commissioner' (PCC). The PCC role was transferred to the Mayor of London in January 2012.These elected commissioners will not run the police, but are intended to 'hold Chief Constables and their forces to account' for policing in their area. Government information on this new role offers this outline:

> PCCs will be responsible for setting the police force's strategic priorities, cutting crime, appointing and, if necessary, dismissing the Chief Constable, and ensuring that policing is efficient and effective.
> (Home Office Information Booklet (2011), 'Police and Crime Commissioners. Have you got what it takes?')

The role of Police and Crime Commissioners is a new innovation in policing, particularly given that the public will elect such individuals (Newburn, 2012). Some critics argue that it will lead to a politicisation of the policing role. See, for example, in Box 2.2, the commentary by Dr Tim Brain, former Gloucestershire Chief Constable and member of the Independent Commission of Policing in England and Wales.

Box 2.2   The big debate – police and crime commissioners

Will directly elected police and crime commissioners give a greater say to the public over policing issues or politicise the delivery of police services?

Bringing direct accountability in the form of police and crime commissioners (PCC) goes some way to bridge the democratic deficit in local policing, but the proposed system is not, however, based on the US model, where commissioners are ultimately answerable to the mayor and more akin to our chief constables.

It is a mishmash of functions and responsibilities and seems an unusual experiment in party politics.

Commissioners will most likely be elected on a party ticket – Conservative, Labour, maybe a few Lib Dems – with the party machine behind them. What's to say x, y, or z won't give them a ring and tell them how they should be thinking? Or to skew policing priorities to more attractive, popular measures that may give them an electoral advantage?

Chief constables have always faced political pressure from politicians, but the ultimate power in policing authorities was dispersed. Now, there will be a risk of more subtle influence: behind closed doors, a PCC may ask a chief constable to focus on a particular local area where the commissioner has a lot of support. And the new PCCs have sole authority to appoint or remove the chief constable. Removing a chief constable is messy, but they will also be on fixed-term contracts, so if you were a young, ambitious chief constable, not quite ready for your pension and your contract was near renewal, what would you do?

Dr Tim Brain, *The Guardian*, 16 April 2012; see http://www.guardian.co.uk/public-leaders-network/2012/apr/16/big-debate-police-crime-commissioners

In Scotland, there are eight regional police forces. Under the *Police (Scotland) Act, 1967*, legal responsibility for policing is shared between Scottish ministers, police authorities and chief constables. In Northern Ireland, the Police Service of Northern Ireland (PSNI) is a single force with one chief constable and it covers the whole jurisdiction. In Box 2.3 there is a list of some of the core policing functions. The role of the police and policing is discussed more fully in Chapter 3.

Box 2.3   Agency functions: police

- Preventing crime
- Investigating crime
- Arresting and detaining suspects
- Maintaining public order
- Protecting the public from terrorist threats
- Traffic control
- Responding to criminal and non-criminal emergencies

Prosecution Service

After a suspect has been charged the case is then taken over by a separate prosecution service. In England and Wales, this is the Crown Prosecution Service (CPS), a state agency independent of the police, which was created by the *Prosecution of Offences Act, 1985*. In Northern Ireland, the Public Prosecution Service (PPS) (established in 2005) carries out a similar function, and in Scotland the Crown Office and Procurator Fiscal Service (COPFS) conducts the prosecution of criminal cases.

The rationale for having separate prosecution services is that they provide legal expertise and are independent from the police. On receiving the file of evidence in a case the prosecution service will review the material and make a decision on whether to proceed to prosecution, based on two main critieria:

1. There is sufficient evidence in the case to result in a reasonable prospect of conviction;
2. That the prosecution is in the public interest.

These two principal criteria are referred to respectively as the 'evidential test' and the 'public interest' test (the application of these tests is discussed in more detail in Chapter 4). If these criteria are not met, the case will not proceed to prosecution. If the prosecution criteria are met, the case can generally proceed to the next stage of the process, which is court. In certain instances provisions exist that allow for other measures to be taken, for example, cautioning an offender or diversion from court towards an alternative scheme (e.g. restorative justice). Such alternatives are used mostly for children and young people (this topic is discussed more fully in Chapter 7). In Scotland, the prosecution agency, the Crown Office and Procurator Fiscal Service (COPFS), also has the authority to impose a direct measure such as a fine, and in such instances the case will not proceed to court.

Box 2.4   Agency functions: prosecution services

- Deciding if cases should proceed to prosecution
- Preparing cases for prosecution
- Prosecution of cases in courts and liaising with other legal professionals re prosecution

---

The courts

There are some significant differences in the structuring of the courts and the terminology used in different courts in the constituent jurisdictions of the United Kingdom (these will be discussed more fully in Chapter 4).

Nonetheless some general overarching principles apply. Firstly, while dependent on other agencies within the criminal justice system for their caseload, the courts are independent from all other agencies within the criminal justice system and also, importantly, from the political process. The so-called 'separation of powers' is one of the fundamental principles of many democratic states:

this means that the courts and judiciary should be free from political interference or persuasion. A criminal case should theoretically be decided based on the evidence presented and not take into account extraneous factors such as a political debate or opinion on a particular case or types of cases.

Secondly, the criminal justice process in the United Kingdom is based on an *adversarial* model of justice. This means that the parties in the case typically a 'defendant' and 'victim' are pitted against each other. The prosecution service, which prosecutes the case on behalf of the state (and, interestingly, not on behalf of the victim, who may be the injured party), sets out to present evidence to the court that will prove *beyond reasonable doubt* that the defendant is guilty. The defence counsel (the legal representative of the defendant) can challenge this evidence through a variety of means, including cross-examining the prosecution's witnesses and presenting alternative evidence to the court. Ultimately the decision-maker within the court – and who this is varies according to court level and jurisdiction: in some instances it may be a jury (e.g. Crown Court in England and Wales) or in others a Sheriff (Sheriff Court in Scotland) – will decide the guilt or otherwise of the defendant based on the evidence presented.

The question of guilt is not one of half-measures. In this system in order to be found guilty the prosecution must prove the guilt of the defendant *beyond reasonable doubt.* This is termed the 'burden of proof', and the responsibility for adequately providing this proof rests with the prosecution. This distinguishes criminal courts from civil courts (which deal with private law matters, e.g. divorce proceedings), where the evidential standard is based on the 'balance of probabilities'.

Because the criminal justice court process is adversarial, the facts of the case may be hotly disputed. This is not always the case. For example, the defendant may plead guilty at an early stage and therefore a degree of consensus is reached. However, the adversarial system has been criticised because of its potentially divisive nature. Many victims' advocates have argued that such a system potentially retraumatises victims, for example, through rigorous cross-examination in the witness box (Bottoms & Roberts, 2010). Furthermore, unlike *inquisitorial systems* (such as those in many European countries), the adversarial system is not about conducting a court inquiry; it is about hearing the evidence presenting and coming to a finding. In this sense the adversarial court is reliant on the evidence presented to it by the two opposing parties.

Finally, the court systems of the United Kingdom are organised hierarchically. There are lower and higher courts. Typically lower courts hear cases of a less serious nature, and their powers of sentencing (i.e. the severity of the penalty they can impose) are less than those of the higher courts. If a person wishes to appeal a conviction or sentence there is a process to be followed, and if the appeal is granted, this will be heard by a higher court.

Box 2.5 Agency functions: the courts

- Handling and processing cases efficiently
- Deciding on bail, remands and mode of trial
- Protecting the rights of the defendant
- Deciding on guilt
- Passing sentence
- Hearing appeals against conviction and sentence
- Providing a public arena so that justice can be seen to be done

---

Sentencing

Following conviction the court proceeds to sentence. Before deciding on the sentence the court can request a pre-sentence report from a probation officer (or criminal justice social workers in Scotland). A pre-sentence report is intended to provide information to the court to assist the sentencing process, and will contain information on the offender's background, including their social circumstances and reasons for committing the offence. The report also typically contains an assessment of risk of reoffending and risk of serious harm. Such assessments are informed by interviews with the offender, information on the circumstances of the current offence, any previous convictions and any other relevant indicators, for example, ongoing substance misuse issues. The pre-sentence report author will consider the sentencing options available to the court and assess the offender's suitability for a community disposal (e.g. unpaid work in the community), if appropriate. The court is not bound by the proposal made in the report, but will take this information into consideration when passing sentence.

The most common court disposal is a fine. Figure 2.1 provides an overview of sentences issued by the court in England and Wales in the 12-month period September 2010–September 2011. It illustrates that fines constituted almost two-thirds of all disposals in this period; the next most common sentence was a community sentence (13 per cent). Prison was proportionately one of the least common sentences (7 per cent).[4]

Probation services/criminal justice social work

Alongside the preparation of pre-sentence reports, probation services (or criminal justice social workers in Scotland) are also responsible for the supervision of community sentences imposed by the courts. There is a range of community sentences available in the various jurisdictions, including community service orders (unpaid work in the community) and probation orders. When subject to

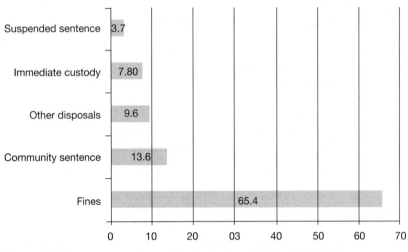

Figure 2.1 Court sentences imposed in England and Wales, 2010–2011

a probation order an offender is required to report on a regular basis to the supervising probation officer and undertake work to address the causes of their offending. This can include, for example, a requirement to attend a group-work programme or to engage with substance misuse services. Such orders are for a specified period of time set by the court, and the probation worker can return the person to court if they are not complying with the terms of their order.

In addition to the supervision of community sentences, probation services also have a responsibility to supervise offenders when they are released from custody 'on licence'. In England and Wales, probation services are delivered at a local area level via Probation Trusts. The headquarters of the probation and the prison services in England and Wales were brought together in 2008 under a newly established executive agency of the Ministry for Justice: the *National Offender Management Service (NOMS)*. In Northern Ireland, probation services are operated by a separate body, the Probation Board for Northern Ireland (PBNI), while in Scotland Criminal Justice Social Workers fulfil a similar role in local authorities (this is discussed in detail in Chapter 5).

Box 2.6   Agency functions: probation/criminal justice social work

- Preparing pre-sentence reports
- Supervising released prisoners and pre-released work with prisoners in custody
- Supervision of community orders

Prison services

As the sentencing snapshot from England and Wales illustrates, prison is used proportionately less than other penalties, but nonetheless the rising rate of imprisonment in England and Wales has been a source of concern. In 2012, the rate of imprisonment in England and Wales was 155 per 100,000 people. The rates of imprisonment for Scotland and Northern Ireland were 157 and 99 per 100,000 respectively.[5] The use of imprisonment and issues around the variation in rates over time is discussed more fully in Chapter 6. Similar to the other agencies in the criminal justice system discussed so far, there are separate prison services in England and Wales, Scotland and Northern Ireland. Across the jurisdictions the core functions of prisons are broadly similar and are outlined in Box 2.7.

Box 2.7   Agency functions: prisons

- Holding persons remanded in custody by the courts
- Holding sentenced offenders
- Punishment and rehabilitation of offenders

A separate criminal justice system for young people?

So far we have discussed the criminal justice system as it operates for adults. There are distinct criminal justice processes and systems for young people (i.e. those under the age of 18). In England, Wales and Northern Ireland, the age of criminal responsibility is 10 years. In Scotland, the age of criminal responsibility is 8 years, but under legislation passed in 2010, a child under the age of 12 years cannot be prosecuted for an offence.[6] For young people in these age categories a separate justice system applies. This is usually referred to as the Youth Justice System. There are some features of commonality with the adult system, but in recognition of age overall the sentences available are less severe and some separate philosophies apply. The rationale for a separate criminal justice system for young people and the contours of the various systems are discussed in Chapter 7.

Conclusion

There are few institutions more central to modern society than a criminal justice system, with the inherent tensions and challenges it faces in delivering a fair and effective service. In this chapter we have suggested that in order to understand how the criminal justice system operates it is necessary to identify its many aims and constituent parts. This chapter has demonstrated that as a system the criminal justice system is not seamless. The question – what is the criminal justice system for? – is a critical one to consider. We have illustrated that the purposes of the criminal justice system can shift, and rationales can ebb and flow both across time and as a person moves through the criminal justice process. The following chapters consider these issues in more depth as we proceed to explore the context and patterning of the criminal justice system over time and across the jurisdictions of the United Kingdom.

Glossary

Due process – Is the principle that the government must respect all of the legal rights that are owed to a person according to the law.

'Just deserts' – The literal meaning of this term is: getting what you deserve. It is used in criminal justice terms to refer to a sentence that is proportionate to the crime committed.

Police and Crime Commissioners (PCC) – this is a newly established role within the criminal justice system in England and Wales. PCCs will be elected by the public and will work to formulate policing and crime reduction targets in their local areas.

Remand – to order an accused person to be kept in custody or placed on bail pending a further court appearance. The word derives from the Latin *remandare*, meaning 'to send back word' or 'to repeat a command'.

Law – Law is a system of rules, usually enforced through a set of institutions. It shapes politics, economics and society in numerous ways and serves as a primary social mediator of relations between people. Contract law regulates everything from buying a bus ticket to trading on derivatives markets.

Case study

The Naked Rambler

Stephen Gough is currently serving a prison sentence for breach of the peace and contempt of court. He attracted media attention (and the attention of the criminal justice system) and was labelled 'the Naked Rambler' when he attempted to walk naked from Lands End to John O'Groats in 2006. He was charged and has served a succession of prison sentences for his determination to walk naked. His last sentence to prison followed his release, when he left Perth prison in Scotland naked and was charged with a breach of the peace, and he appeared in court naked and was charged with being in contempt of the court. As *The Guardian* reported in a profile of Gough in March 2012:

In Scotland, breach of the peace is partly defined as 'conduct which does, or could, cause the lieges [public] to be placed in a state of fear, alarm or annoyance'. The prosecution has very rarely managed to rustle up witnesses to claim Gough's nakedness has had any of these effects on them. What is keeping him in prison is simply the theoretical idea that it could.

'The Naked Rambler: The man prepared to go to prison for nudity', *The Guardian*, 23 March 2012

Gough's latest conviction is his seventeenth in ten years – all for similar offences. He has been assessed on numerous occasions and is not mentally ill. The question of why the criminal justice system is mobilised to stop Gough's behaviour is a relevant one – What is the criminal justice system for? What is so offensive of about a person who wishes to walk naked, and why is the criminal justice system employed to stop him?

Seminar questions

1. Can we describe the criminal justice system as a system or as a process?
2. What purpose is the criminal justice system intended to serve?
3. Discuss in groups as to whether the criminal justice system can deliver justice in a fair and effective way.

Further information can be obtained from the following websites

Government legislation: All legislation enacted in the UK from 1267 to the present, including the legislation of the different regional parliaments, can be accessed via this website: http://www.legislation.gov.uk/. A useful search function on the site allows you to see which geographical regions the legislation pertains to.

Court systems: The website of the Courts and Tribunal Service in Northern Ireland provides a comprehensive overview of the court structure and process in this jurisdiction. Information is also provided on legal judgments: http://www.courtsni.gov.uk/

The website of the Scottish Courts provides similar resources: http://www.scotcourts.gov.uk/

Information on courts in England and Wales can be obtained from the website of HM Courts and Tribunals Service: http://www.justice.gov.uk/about/hmcts

Prison systems worldwide: Information on prison systems and populations from different countries across the world, including the United Kingdom, is available from the International Centre for Prison Studies' website: http://www.prisonstudies.org/

Further reading

Ellis, T. & Savage, S. (2011) *Debates in Criminal Justice.* London: Routledge
This book provides an overview of some of key debates in criminal justice practice. It includes discussions on the adversarial system of justice and the role of prisons within the criminal justice system.

Maguire, M., Morgan, R. & Reiner, R. (eds) (2012) *The Oxford Handbook of Criminology*, 5th edn. Oxford: Oxford University Press
This handbook contains chapters on various aspects of the criminal justice system. In includes political, sociological and psychological perspectives on crime as well as detailed analyses on the operation of different parts of the criminal justice system.

Zedner, L. (2004) *Criminal Justice.* Clarendon Law Series. Oxford: Oxford University Press
This book provides an accessible overview of some of the theories and rationales that underpin the criminal justice system.

References

Bottoms, A. & Roberts, J. (2010) (eds) *Hearing the Victim: Adversarial Justice, Crime Victims and the State.* Cullompton: Willan Publishing

Brownlee, I. (1998) *Community Punishment: A Critical Introduction.* Harlow: Longman

Croall, H. (2006) 'Criminal justice in post-devolutionary Scotland', *Critical Social Policy*, 26, 3: 587–607

Ellis, T. & Savage, S. (2011) *Debates in Criminal Justice.* London: Routledge

Ellison, G. & Mulcahy, A. (2009) 'Crime and criminal justice in Northern Ireland'. In: A. Huckelsby & A. Wahidin (eds) *Criminal Justice.* Oxford: Oxford University Press, pp. 313–33.

Morgan, R. & Liebling, A. (2007) 'Imprisonment: An expanding scene'. In: M. Maguire, R. Morgan & R. Reiner (eds) *The Oxford Handbook of Criminology*, 4th edn. Oxford: Oxford University Press, pp. 1100–39

Newburn, T. (2012) 'Police and Crime Commissioners: The Americanization of policing or a very British reform?', *International Journal of Law and Criminal Justice*, 40, 1: 31–45

Sanders, A. & Young, R. (2000) *Criminal Justice*, 2nd edn. London: Butterworth

Uglow, S., Dickson, L., Cheney, D. & Doolin, K. (2002) *Criminal Justice.* London: Sweet & Maxwell

Ward, T. & Maruna, S. (2007) *Rehabilitation.* London: Routledge

Wilson, D. & Ashton, J. (2001) *What Everyone in Britain Should Know About Crime and Punishment*, 2nd edn. Oxford: Oxford University Press

Young, J. & Matthews, R. (2003) 'New Labour, crime control and social exclusion'. In R. Matthews & J. Young (eds) *The New Politics of Crime and Punishment.* Cullompton: Willan Publishing, pp. 1–33

Zedner, L. (2004) *Criminal Justice.* Clarendon Law Series. Oxford: Oxford University Press

3 Police and policing

Key issues

- Explain the role of the police.
- What is the difference between 'the police' and 'policing'?
- Explain the changing nature of policing.

Introduction

The title of this chapter highlights problems of definition in writing about the police and policing history. In tracing the development of policing, this chapter will show that although the police have been described at times as *protectors, domestic missionaries, pigs and pariahs*, the police are an inevitable fact of modern society. Everyone has an intuitive notion of what the police are and what they do. However, to understand the nature and role of policing, especially over space and time, requires some conceptual exploration of the taken-for-granted idea of the police, which therefore needs to be unpacked. This chapter will introduce you to some of the key areas in the development of the police in England and Wales. It will start with by defining the difference between the police and policing, explore the role and development of the police and police accountability, and look at the organisation of the police today.

It is important to distinguish between the ideas of 'police' and 'policing'. The idea of policing is an aspect of social control, and in turn is a set of activities directed at preserving the security of a particular social order through sur-veillance and the threat of punishment (Cohen & Scull, 1983). Policing, as Reiner (2000: 3) argues, is 'a set of activities of a particular social order in general'. Policing may be carried out by a multitude of people and techniques, of which the modern conception of the 'police' is only one. While policing may be universal, the 'police' as a specialised body of people given the primary respon-sibility for legitimate force to safeguard security is a feature only of relatively complex societies. Policing refers to 'organised forms of order-maintenance, peace-keeping, rule or law enforcement, crime investigation and prevention and other forms of investigation and information-brokering' (Jones & Newburn, 1998: 18).

Let's turn our attention to the 'police'. The police are not found in every society – they are a specialised, state-organised body that has a broad mandate, performing a variety of tasks to keep the peace (without always resorting to legal proceedings). Broadly, their work focuses on crime control, order maintenance and service work, from traffic control to terrorism (Reiner, 2000). However, ultimately the police have the power to invoke legal sanctions. 'A benign bobby . . . still brings to the situation a uniform, a truncheon, and a battery of resource charges . . . which can be employed when appeasement fails and fists start flying' (Punch, 1979: 116).

History of policing: the birth of the blues

Before the nineteenth century, no organisation was responsible for policing, and, as Brogden *et al.* (1988) point out, the array of functions was carried out by a hotchpotch of different arrangements. Some parishes employed watchmen, and other policing functions were carried out privately. Towards the end of the eighteenth century the novelist, police reformer and lawyer Henry Fielding with his brother, John Fielding, established the Bow Street Runners, which consisted of 12 men (Emsley, 2010). Sir Robert Peel established the police force in England and Wales in 1828, and it was his previous role as Chief Secretary for Ireland (between 1812 and 1818) that influenced his approach to policing in London. Fielding was instrumental in the passing of the Dublin Police Act, 1786 and Peel in the creation of the Peace Preservation force in 1814 (Palmer, 1988). By 1828 'The New Police' were established in England and by 1836 the Metropolitan Police was formed.

The idea of the *'New Police'* implies that an *'old'* police had previously existed. The 'newness' consisted of the institution of a bureaucratic organisation of professionals, rationally administered and directed towards a policy of 'preventative policing', that is, regular patrols to deter crime, suppress disorder and maintain security. The 'newness' of the Metropolitan Police was also reflected in the entry standards and discipline established by Peel and the first two Metropolitan Commissioners he appointed: Colonel Charles Rowan (of the Light Brigade) and Richard Mayne, a barrister. Rowan and Mayne put in place a strict set of rules and regulations governing not only the standards of dress, deportment and discipline, but how to conduct oneself when dealing with the public. These were inculcated during drill and training, and individuals were punished for acts of disobedience. A chain of command was instituted, and at first the policy was to appoint former non-commissioned military officers to the higher ranks, because of their experience as disciplinarians. This later changed in favour of internal promotion from the ranks (Wall, 1998).

By 1837 the new police were 'universally accepted', becoming a 'domestic missionary' (Storch, 1975, 1976) and 'the moral entrepreneur of public property' (Cohen, 1979: 128). However, the emergence of the police was protracted and at times fiercely contested. As Storch (1975) clearly outlines, the police were seen as 'unproductive parasites' (in the sense that police work was not seen as 'real' work), described by an array of derogatory epithets such as: 'Crushers', 'Peel's Bloody Gang', 'A Plague of Blue Locusts', 'Jenny Darbies', 'Raw Lobsters' and 'Blue Drones' (Critchley, 1970; Storch, 1975). Yet by the 1950s the police had become not merely accepted but were seen as a symbol of national pride (Loader, 1997). However, by the latter half of the twentieth century, a series of police scandals, including corruption and miscarriages of justice; race and sex discrimination; deaths in police custody, the rise of paramilitary policing in managing public disorder and most recently the revelations from the Leveson Inquiry (ongoing),[1] has called into question the legitimacy of the police. Although public opinion began to change, the police still remain central symbols of security in the eyes of many (Loader & Mulcahy, 2003).

The organisation of the police

Although this chapter will focus on England and Wales, it is important to recognise variations in the different jurisdictions – that is, policing in Scotland and Northern Ireland. The first major police force created in Scotland was in Glasgow under the Glasgow Police Act 1800, almost thirty years earlier than the establishment of the Metropolitan Police. The motto of the Scottish police Service is *Semper Vigilo,* implying a vigilance for the safety of Scottish society and the people of Scotland (Dinsmor & Goldsmith, 2005; Donnelly & Scott, 2005). The laws of Scotland played a determining role in defining the crimes, offences and police duties. The *Police (Scotland) Act, 1967* remains the chief legal cornerstone for Scottish policing.

It could be argued that the single most important change in Scotland in recent times has been the *Scotland Act, 1998*, the legislation that brought about constitutional devolution. As a part of Scotland's domestic affairs, policing lies within the remit of a devolved parliament and Scottish Executive/ Government, not Westminster (Dinsmor & Goldsmith, 2005; Donnelly & Scott, 2005). Policing in Scotland shares similarities with other parts of the UK although there are clear variations, drawing on certain legal and historical traditions, which differentiate it significantly especially in light of Scottish devolution (McFadden & Lazarowitcz, 2002).

The history of policing in Northern Ireland is complex and is tied indelibly to the context of political conflict. Until Direct Rule from Westminster was introduced in 1972, the Protestant-based Ulster Unionist Party had ruled Northern Ireland continuously for over half a century under stringent emergency legislation (Ellison & Smyth, 2000). The Royal Ulster Constabulary (RUC), which itself had been in operation since the disbandment of the Royal Irish Constabulary in 1922, was supported by The Ulster Special Constabulary (also known as the 'B' Specials), and by an extensive range of legislative powers (most notably, the Civil Authorities (Special Powers) Act, 1923). The RUC was heavily criticised for the heavy-handed and partisan manner in which its officers suppressed nationalist dissent and policed the civil rights movement (Cameron Committee, 1969: 72–4), including indiscriminate use of gunfire resulting in civilian deaths, which was further demonstrated by a clear 'failure to prevent Protestant mobs from burning Catholic houses' and 'the failure to take every effective action to restrain or disperse mobs, or to protect lives and property' (Scarman Tribunal, 1972: 15).

Against this backdrop and a lack of confidence in the delivery of policing in Northern Ireland, a policing reform agenda was set in place under the terms of the Good Friday Agreement 1998. The Commission, chaired by Chris Patten, published what became known as *The Patten Report*, making a total of 175 recommendations. The publication of the report led to the disbandment of the Royal Ulster Constabulary and the establishment of the Police Service of Northern Ireland (PSNI). Alongside the name change a range of reforms and oversight mechanisms were introduced, including the Policing Board, District Policing Partnerships and the Police Ombudsman (Ellison *et al.*, 2012). The Oversight Commissioner noted that: 'The recommendations of the Patten Commission and the success of the Police Service of Northern Ireland in implementing them are now being seen as models for many police forces around the world' (Office of the Oversight Commissioner, 2003: 1).

Policing in England and Wales

With a brief outline of the different contexts that policing occurs in, the following section will focus on 'the police' in England and Wales. There are presently 43 forces,[2] which comprise more than 243,000 police staff, 143,000 full officers, special constables and community support officers (CSOs). Staff account for about 80 per cent of all police spending (Flanagan, 2008). The Metropolitan Police is the largest police force, with almost 31,000 officers and a further 14,000 civilian staff. In addition to the 43 forces, there are a number of 'non-Home Office' police forces that have a specialised remit and exercise their jurisdiction throughout the UK. These include the British Transport Police (BTP); the Ministry of Defence Police (MOD); the United Kingdom Atomic Energy Authority Police; and the Ministry of Defence Police. The Jersey, Guernsey and Isle of Man Police are separate organisations that carry out policing in those islands.

Figure 3.1 A fortified police vehicle still used by the police in Northern Ireland
Source: © Wahidin, A. (2011)

Roles and responsibilities

The current system of holding 43 forces of England and Wales accountable has been characterised as 'the tripartite structure of police accountability'. This structure was established under the *Police Act, 1964*, following the recommendations of the 1962 Royal Commission on the Police and the *Police and Magistrates Court Act, 1994*, consolidated as the *Police Act, 1996*. The 1964 Act created the tripartite system of accountability for the current provincial forces in England and Wales, distributing responsibilities between the Home Office, the Home Secretary, the local police authority and the chief constable of the force. This model remains the fundamental basis of police governance. However, the two London forces, the Metropolitan and the City of London force, differ from this pattern.

As the previous chapter has outlined, under new government proposals, from November 2012 each police force in England and Wales will have a publicly elected 'Police and Crime Commissioner' (PCC). These elected commissioners are intended to 'hold Chief Constables and their forces to account' for policing in their area. However, as the following section of this chapter discusses, the questions of accountability and transparency of policing are ones that have dogged the police and have been brought into particular sharp focus by a series of scandals.

Accountability

To address the issue of police accountability, the 1981 Royal Commission on Criminal Procedure Report (RCCP) led to *The Police and Criminal Evidence Act, 1984 (PACE)*. The RCCP focused on the rights of suspects, an issue that had been debated for some time, but which had been brought to a head by the 'Confait Case', in which three boys had been convicted of murder on the basis of false confessions (see Box 3.1).

Box 3.1   'The Confait case'

In 1972 two boys made confessions to the police at a police station that they had murdered Maxwell Confait at his home in southeast London. A third boy also admitted to setting fire to a house to destroy evidence. The boys, aged 18, 15 and 14, were found guilty of these offences and spent three years in custody before a successful appeal led to their release. A subsequent report of an inquiry into the case, the *Fisher Report* (1978), criticised the manner in which the police had obtained confessions from the young people, one of whom had a learning disability. The Fisher Report

---

itself was controversial, however, because of some of the conclusions reached by its author, Sir Henry Fisher, regarding the guilt of the defendants based on a 'balance of probabilities' (McBarnet, 1978). However, the findings of the report ultimately led to the establishment of the *Royal Commission on Criminal Procedure* in 1978 and the recommendations for rules regarding police evidence and the establishment of a separate prosecution service in England and Wales (see further, Chapter 4).

The purpose for the introduction of the *Police and Criminal Evidence Act, 1984 (PACE)* was to rationalise and modernise the law governing police powers, and to provide a balance of police powers and safeguards for suspects. The safeguards are set out by the Act itself and in the Codes of Practice accompanying it. PACE sought to overcome the problem of the low visibility of police work by requiring that each exercise of a power had to be recorded.[3] For example, Section 1 extended the power to stop and search, but this must be grounded in 'reasonable suspicion', with a written record as soon as possible, and made available to the suspect. All the safeguards are underpinned by Section 67 of PACE, which makes failure to comply with them a disciplinary offence.

In addition, PACE includes sections purporting to enhance police accountability more generally, for example, through the complaints process and by community consultation. PACE not only extended police powers in a number of important ways but also introduced far-reaching procedural safeguards (some of which were revised in 1991 and again subsequently). Thus guarding against abuse of police powers included, for example, ensuring that all interviews in police stations are tape-recorded, and that in order to convict a court has to be sure that an offence has been committed and that the evidence to prove this is admissible. It is reasonable to argue that the Act has had an impact on the behaviour of police officers, and on the culture of policing.

Although PACE has achieved some standardisation in police practice, widespread powers have been given to the police by subsequent Acts, such as the *Public Order Act, 1986*, the *Criminal Justice and Public Order Act (CJPOA), 1994*, the *Proceeds of Crime Act, 2002*, the *Criminal Justice Act, 2003*, the *Serious Organised Crime Act, 2005* and other statutes. Thus PACE has been amended and cannot be seen as the only code of police powers in place (Dixon, 1997).

Policing scandals

Alongside a series of miscarriages of justice (some of which are discussed in the following chapter), the most persistent complaints of police violence and harassment came from black and minority ethnic communities, which was one of the many reasons behind the inner-city riots of 1981 and 1985, in Toxteth in Liverpool and Brixton in London. Leading up to the riots, McNee (1979) proposed that a wide-ranging study be carried out on the relations between the Metropolitan Police and the community: the resulting report by the Policy Studies Institute made uncomfortable reading on the subject of race relations. The researchers found: 'that racist language and racial prejudice were prominent and pervasive and that individual officers and also whole groups were preoccupied with ethnic differences'. While this did not necessarily prevent friendly relations between the police and the black community, the researchers concluded that 'police hostility towards people of West Indian origin is connected with the belief that they are rootless, alienated, poor, unable to cope and deviant in various ways' (Smith & Gray, 1983: 55).

The outcome of the Brixton riots and the way it was policed and managed led to an inquiry headed by Lord Scarman, who was critical of the way the police carried out an operation known as 'Swamp 81', a 'street saturation' operation in which more than half the people who were stopped were black. Scarman's recommendations were far-reaching and addressed the recruitment of ethnic minorities, the use of liaison committees to build better relationships with the police and local communities, introducing lay visitors to police stations, creating an independent review of complaints against the police and the tightening of regulations regarding racially prejudiced behaviour by officers. However, even though the Scarman Report (1981) did bring about change, a little over a decade after the Scarman Inquiry, on 22 April 1993, Stephen Lawrence, an 18-year-old, was stabbed to death while standing at a bus in an unprovoked racist attack, giving rise to another significant police inquiry (Bowling 1999; Macpherson, 1999; and see case study at the end of this chapter).

The Stephen Lawrence Inquiry concluded, in contrast to Scarman, that: 'the investigation was marred by a combination of professional incompetence, institutional racism and a *failure* of leadership by senior officers' (1999: para. 46.1, emphasis added). In his report Scarman rejected the concept of 'institutional racism' as an explanation of the problems that had precipitated the inquiry. However, he did state that if: 'the suggestion being made is that practices may be adopted by public bodies as well as private individuals which are *unwittingly discriminatory* against black people, then this allegation which deserves serious consideration, and, where proved, swift remedy' (Scarman, 1982: para 2.22, emphasis added). These revelations of the falsification of evidence to secure a conviction, corruption and the failure to deliver public protection from crime in an equitable way challenged the identity and legitimacy of the police (Punch, 2009).

The outcome of the Stephen Lawrence Inquiry is that it has left a lasting impression on policing that goes beyond the processes of the investigative practice. The 70 recommendations made, almost all of which were accepted by the government, amounted to the most extensive programme of reform both in terms of policy and policing practices. For example, it has led to the production of the 'Murder Investigation Manual' (ACPO, 2006) and the Major Incident Room Standardised Administrative Procedures or 'MIRSAP' (Neyroud & Disley, 2007), with recommended improvements in training, recruitment and the handling of racist incidents. It has been described: 'as the most extensive programme of reform in the history of the relationship between the police and ethnic minority communities' (Bowling & Phillips, 2002: 16; Rowe, 2007) and, as Reiner (2000: 211) suggests,

> the Macpherson Report . . . has transformed the terms of the political debate about black people and criminal justice . . . what had not [previously] featured in public awareness and political debate was the disproportionate rate at which black people suffered as victims of crime.

Although there is some debate as to the extent of reform in the aftermath of 'post-Lawrence', the number of stop and searches fell from all-time high in 1998 of around one million to around three-quarters of a million in 2002. This curtailment is due to changes in stop and search powers. There were 45,932 stops and searches by police in England, Scotland and Wales under Section 44 of the Terrorism Act, 2000 in the year ended September 2010 – a 77 per cent reduction on the previous 12 months, when there were 200,775, according to Home Office figures. The largest reduction in use of Section 44 powers was by the Metropolitan Police, from 152,378 in 2009 to 39,236 in 2010. The use of Section 44 powers fell most dramatically after July 2010, when the Home Secretary, Theresa May, scrapped their use against individuals, in line with a European court ruling that they were unlawful (Rowland, 2004).

A representative force?

The question of the representativeness of police forces has also been raised in the range of landmark reports including the aforementioned Scarman, Macpherson and Patten reports. In the Northern Ireland context, one of the impetuses for the disbandment of the Royal Ulster Constabulary and the establishment of the PSNI was the fact that the RUC was not seen to be representative of both communities (i.e. Protestant and Catholic). Following the Patten reforms a recruitment quota was introduced in order to try to recruit more Catholics into what had been seen as a Protestant police force (Ellison & Smyth, 2000).

Over the past decade in England and Wales there have also been numerous attempts to increase the representation of women and minority ethnic groups within the police service. The proportion of female officers has been increasing, with women now comprising 23 per cent of police service strength. Women still tend to be concentrated in the lower ranks, and the number of women officers resigning has been twice as high as for men. Women make up 33 per cent of special constables, 42 per cent of police service civilian staff (including traffic wardens) and 66 per cent of police community support officers (Flanagan, 2008). However, only 12 per cent of chief police officers are female (ibid.), and the first female Chief Constable, Pauline Clare, was not appointed until 1995.

Similarly, there have been considerable efforts made to recruit members from minority ethnic groups, which currently stand at 4 per cent of overall police numbers (see Table 3.1) and 7 per cent of the Metropolitan Police Service.

The next step for policing

The final section will explore the increasing use of other agencies in delivering broadly defined policing activities through the commodification of aspects of private security. Moreover, the increasing role of the privatisation of policing by the private security sector is directing the future of police work and changing the very nature of policing. Policing has many possible futures and, indeed, it is impossible to predict what the 'future' really holds. However, in thinking about the changing landscape of the police, policing appears to have become fragmented, and the police as we know it is being replaced by a pluralised assortment of bodies with policing functions. The key changes that mark this period are characterised by:

Table 3.1 Police officer strength: England and Wales, 2001–2010

	Total, excluding secondments	Of which: Female number	Female %	Of which: Minority ethnic[13] number	Minority ethnic %	Total strength[14]
2001	123,476	21,174	17.1%	2,955	2.4%	125,682
2002	127,267	22,784	17.9%	3,362	2.6%	129,603
2003	131,426	25,139	19.1%	3,868	2.9%	133,366
2004	137,105	26,956	19.7%	4,594	3.3%	139,200
2005	139,491	28,898	20.7%	4,971	3.5%	141,230
2006	139,631	30,307	21.7%	5,236	3.7%	141,381
2007	140,032	31,914	22.8%	5,519	3.9%	140,514
2008	139,728	32,861	23.5%	5,793	4.1%	140,230
2009	141,647	34,651	24.5%	6,290	4.4%	142,151
Sept. 2009	142,209	n/a	n/a	n/a	n/a	142,688
2010	141,674	35,434	25.0%	6,642	4.6%	142,175
Sept. 2010	139,740	n/a	n/a	n/a	n/a	140,253

Source: *Amended Home Office Statistical Bulletin, Police Service Strength, England and Wales*

1. The increasing public/private permeability has led to changing patterns in police work, and the private sector is increasingly making incursions into the public-run police service.
2. The pluralising of policing – or, as Bayley and Shearing put it, 'the end of a monopoly' by the public police (Bayley & Shearing, 1996: 38), has led to an emergence and a proliferation of a variety of commercial, private and non-public forms of policing. For example, we are routinely placed in positions where private security personnel may search us (airport security), exclude us (shopping malls), place us under surveillance (CCTV) and in night clubs, the bouncers can evict us.
3. Policing within in and between nation states.

Bayley and Shearing state that: 'future generations will look back on our era as a time when one system of policing ended and another took its place' (1996: 585). The extent to which perceived changes in policing have seen the sociology of policing shift form a preoccupation with the police to a broader concern with policing can be debated (see Johnston & Shearing, 2002; Zedner, 2006). But the profound changes in social structure, culture, crime and public order in an age of increasing global interdependence and risk are bound to have implications for the policing that seeks to regulate. The focus of current attention has begun to move away from 'policing' *per se* to the role of 'security networks' (Johnston, 2000), and, indeed, of the 'commodification' of security and that of private policing.

Conclusion

In this chapter we have endeavoured to outline the contours of the development of the police, how they are organised, their role, the decline in public confidence in the police, and how they are made accountable in late modern society. The day-to-day practice of public policing has been influenced by the profes-sionalisation of policing (Weinberger, 1995). Policing has been shaped by human rights legislation (APA, 2008), and by how aspects of policing and security have become increasingly privatised (McMullen, 1996). This raises further questions, as to what will influence the 'new face' of policing: will it be that of police powers, a diverse workforce, rationalisation, marketisation of crime control and becoming more open to the public through consultation of various kinds? The development of partnerships with community-based and private forms of provision is changing the nature of the police and that of policing, expanding its role and creating alternative forms of policing as policing becomes ever more pluralistic. These changes in turn will force the police to reassess their role and redefine what they are there to do and with what agencies.

Glossary

Miscarriages of justice – are cases in which individuals have been wrongly convicted of offences.

National Policing Improvement Agency – is a national policing body established to manage and enhance the performance of 43 police forces in England and Wales through the sharing of expert knowledge.

Police Community Support Officers – are uniformed, civilian employees who possess a range of limited and discretionary police powers.

Special Constables – are volunteer uniformed police officers who possess the full powers of a constable and work a minimum of four hours a week.

Case study

The killing of Stephen Lawrence and the Macpherson Report

Stephen Lawrence was born on 13 September 1974 in southeast London. On the evening of 22 April 1993, Stephen and his friend Duwayne Brooks were subjected to an unprovoked racist attack by five white youths in Well Hall Road, Eltham, southeast London. Stephen Lawrence was stabbed twice during the attack and died shortly afterwards. He didn't know his killers and his killers didn't know him.

After the initial investigation, five suspects were arrested but not convicted. It was suggested during the course of that investigation that the murder was racially motivated and that the handling of the case by the police and Crown Prosecution Service had been affected by issues of race. A public inquiry was set up by the then Home Secretary Jack Straw in July 1997. The inquiry was headed by Sir William Macpherson, who examined the original Metropolitan Police Service (MPS) investigation and compiled The Macpherson Report. The report concluded that the force was 'institutionally racist' and that the murder was 'marred by a combination of professional incompetence, institutional racism and a failure of leadership by senior officers (Macpherson, 1999: 34). The publication in 1999 Macpherson Report has been 'the most radical official statement on race, policing and criminal justice ever produced in this country' (McLaughlin, 1993: 13).

On 18 May 2011, it was announced that two of the original suspects, Gary Dobson and David Norris, were to stand trial for the murder in the light of 'new and substantial evidence' becoming available. New scientific evidence, which used much more rigorous testing of the clothing of the five main suspects and of Lawrence, tied Dobson and Norris to the murder

---

and disproved their claims that they were not present during the attack. The change in law on double jeopardy has allowed the prosecution to apply to quash an acquittal if a court is satisfied that there is new and compelling evidence to be put before a jury.

On 3 January 2012, Dobson and Norris were found guilty of Lawrence's murder, and were sentenced on 4 January 2012 to detention at Her Majesty's Pleasure, equivalent to a life sentence for an adult with minimum terms of 15 years 2 months and 14 years 3 months respectively for what the judge described as a 'terrible and evil crime'. The murder brought the issue of race relations and the failure of the police in Britain into sharp focus.

For further details, go to: http://www.guardian.co.uk/Lawrence/Story/0,208692,00.html

Seminar questions

1. Explain the nature of PACE.
2. Can the police offer public protection to all?
3. Explain why women and ethnic minority groups are still unrepresented within the police force.
4. 'Bad apples' or 'rotten barrels?' Discuss in relation to police corruption.

Further information can be obtained from the following websites

Metropolitan Police – http://www.met.police.uk

The main official website for information on policing.

Report of the Stephen Lawrence Inquiry – http://www.archive.officialdocuments. co.uk/document/cm42/4262/4262.htm

Provides online access to the Report.

Home Office (2001) *A Diary of a Police Officer*. Police Research Series Paper 149. Available at http://www.homeoffice.gov.uk/rds/prgpdfs/prs149.pdf

This report provides a detailed insight into the role of the police and police work across England and Wales.

Association of Police Authorities – http://www.apa.police.uk/apa_home.htm
The national voice of police authorities in England, Wales and Northern Ireland.

www.cain.ulst.ac.uk – The Conflict Archive on the Internet website contains a wealth of data on the Northern Ireland criminal justice system.

Further reading

T. Newburn (ed.) (2008a) *Handbook of Policing*, **2nd edn, Cullompton: Willan Publishing**
This is a comprehensive and accessible text that provides a detailed overview of policing in Britain. It examines the issues, debates and transformation in many key areas of the police and policing.

T. Newburn (ed.) (2008b) *Policing Key Readings*, **Cullompton: Willan Publishing**
A comprehensive text that provides key readings examining the history, the role of policing, organisation, culture, the rise of private security and the future of policing.

R. Reiner (2002) *The Politics of the Police*, **3rd edn. Oxford: Oxford University Press**
This remains the most authoritative book on the sociology of policing in Britain.

M. Rowe (ed.) (2007) *Policing Beyond Macpherson*, **Cullompton: Willan Publishing**
The book critically explores the impact of the Lawrence Report on the police service and the extent to which, in retrospect, the Macpherson Inquiry has led to significant changes to policing.

Bibliography

ACPO Centrex (2006) *The Murder Investigation Manual*, 3rd edn. Bedfordshire: Centrix
Association of Police Authorities (APA) (2008) *Human Rights Guidance for Police Authorities, Monitoring Compliance with the Human Rights Act 1998*. London: Association of Police Authorities. Available online at: www.apa.police.uk/
Bayley, D. & Shearing, C. (1996) 'The future of policing', *Law and Society Review*, 30, 3: 585–606
Bowling, B. (1999) *Violent Racism*. Oxford: Oxford University Press
Bowling, B. & Phillips, C. (2002) *Racism, Crime and Justice*. London: Longman
Brogden, M., Jefferdson, T. & Walklate, S. (1988) *Introducing Police Work*. London: Unwin
Cameron, Lord (1969) *Disturbances in Northern Ireland: Report of the Commission, September 1969*. Cmd 532. Belfast: HMSO
Cohen, S. (1979) 'The punitive city', *Contemporary Crises*, 3, 4: 341–63
Cohen, S. & Scull, A. (eds) (1983) *Social Control and the State*. Oxford: Martin Robertson
Critchley, T.A. (1970) *The Conquest of Violence: Order and Liberty in Britain*, London: Constable

Dinsmor, A. & Goldsmith, A. (2005) 'Scottish policing – A historical perspective'. In: D. Donnelly and K. Scott (eds) *Policing Scotland*. Cullompton: Willan Publishing, pp. 40–58

Dixon, D. (1997) *Law in Policing*. Oxford: Oxford University Press

Donnelly, D. & Scott, K. (2002) 'Police accountability in Scotland', *The Police Journal*, 75, 1: 56–66

Ellison, G. & Smyth, J. (2000) *The Crowned Harp: Policing Northern Ireland*. London: Pluto Press

Ellison, G., Shirlow, P. & Mulcahy, A. (2012) 'Responsible participation, community engagement and policing in transitional societies: Lessons from a Local Crime Survey in Northern Ireland'. In: A. Wahidin (ed.) *The Legacy of Conflict and the Impact on the Northern Irish Criminal Justice System, Journal of Howard League for Penal Reform*, 52. London: Blackwell, December

Emsley, C. (2010) *Crime and Society in England 1750–1900*, 4th edn. Harlow: Pearson

Flanagan, Sir Ronnie (2008) *The Review of Policing: Final Report*. London: Home Office

Johnston, L. (1992) 'British policing in the nineties: Free market and strong state?', *International Criminal Justice Review*, 2: 1–18.

Johnston, L. (2000) *Policing Britain, Risk, Security and Governance*. Harlow: Longman

Johnston, L. & Shearing, C. (2002) *Governing Security*. London: Routledge

Jones, T. & Newburn, T. (1998) *Private Security and Public Policing*. Oxford: Oxford University Press

Jones, T. & Newburn, T. (2002) 'The transformation of policing? Understanding current trends in policing systems', *British Journal of Criminology*, 42, 1: 129–46

Johnston, L. & Shearing, C. (2002) *Governing Security*. London: Routledge

Loader, I. (1997) 'Policing and the social: Questions of symbolic power', *British Journal of Sociology*, 48, 1: 1–18

Loader, I. & Mulcahy, A. (2003) *Policing and the Condition of England*. Oxford: Oxford University Press

Macpherson, Sir W. (1999) *The Stephen Lawrence Inquiry, Report of an Inquiry by Sir William Macpherson of Cluny, advised by Tom Cook, The Right Reverend Dr John Sentamu and Dr Richard Stone*. Cm 4262-1. London: The Stationery Office

McBarnet, D. (1978) 'The Fisher Report on the Confait Case: Four issues', *The Modern Law Review*, 41, 4: 455–63

McFadden, J. & Lazarowitcz, M. (2002) *The Scottish Parliament: An Introduction*, 2nd edn. Edinburgh: T. & T. Clark

McLaughlin, E. (1999) 'The search for truth and justice', *Criminal Justice Matters*, 35: 14–17

McMullen, J. (1996) 'The new improved monied police: Reform, crime control, and the commodification of policing in London', *British Journal of Criminology*, 36, 1: 85–108

McNee, D. (1979) 'The Queen's Police keepeth the peace', *Guardian*, 25 September: 25

Newburn, T. (2008) *Handbook of Policing*, 2nd edn. Cullompton: Willan.

Neyroud, P. & Disley, E. (2007) 'The management, supervision and oversight of crime investigation'. In: T. Newburn, T. Williamson & A. Wright (eds) *Handbook of Criminal Investigation*. Cullompton: Willan Publishing, pp. 549–72

Office of the Oversight Commissioner (2003) *Overseeing the Proposed Revisions for the Policing Services of Northern Ireland – Report 8*. 16 September 2003. Belfast: Office of the Oversight Commissioner

Palmer, S.H. (1988) *Police and Protest in England and Ireland 1780–1850*. Cambridge: Cambridge University Press

Punch, M. (1979) 'The secret social service'. In: S. Holdaway (ed.) *The British Police*. London: Edward Arnold, pp. 102–18

Punch, M. (2009) *Police Corruption: Deviance, Accountability, and Reform in Policing*. Cullompton: Willan Publishing

Reiner, R. (2000) *The Politics of the Police*, 4th edn. Oxford: Oxford University Press

Rowe, M. (2007) *Policing Beyond Macpherson: Issues in Policing, Race and Society*. Cullompton: Willan Publishing

Rowland, M. (2004) *The Misuse of Section 44 Stop and Search Powers Continues despite European Court Ruling*. London: Statewatch

Royal Commission on The Police (1962) *Final Report*. Cmnd 1728. London: HMSO

Scarman Tribunal (1972) *Violence and Civil Disturbances in Northern Ireland in 1969: Report of a Tribunal of Inquiry*. Cmnd 566. London: HMSO

Scarman, Lord (1981) *The Scarman Report*. London: HMSO

Scarman, Lord (1982) *The Brixton Disorders*. Cmnd 8427. London: HMSO

Smith, J.D. & Gray, J. (1983) *Police and People in London*. London: Policy Studies Institute

Storch, R. (1975) 'The plague of the blue locusts: Police reform and popular resistance in Northern England 1840–1857', *International Review of Social History*, 20: 1: 61–90

Storch, R. (1976) 'The policeman as domestic missionary: Urban discipline and popular culture in Northern England, 1850–80', *Journal of Social History*, 9, 4: 481–509

Wall, D. (1998) *The Chief Constables of England and Wales*. Aldershot: Dartmouth

Weinberger, B. (1995)*The Best Police in the World*. London: Scholar Press

Zedner, L. (2006) 'Policing before and after the police: The historical antecedents of contemporary crime control', *British Journal of Criminology*, 46, 1: 78–96

4   Prosecution and
the court process

Key issues

- How are decisions made on which cases to prosecute?
- How are the criminal courts structured?
- What happens when justice goes wrong?

Introduction

This chapter discusses the main criminal justice agencies that are involved in the prosecution process. This is a process with a number of phases, including an assessment of the evidence and a decision as to whether prosecution is 'in the public interest'. Prosecution also refers to the court stage whereby defendants are brought to court and possibly tried; a trial does not take place if the defendant enters a guilty plea at an early stage. The court system is organised hierarchically, and the type of court a defendant is tried in will be dependent, among other factors, on the seriousness of the offence. There are variations in the court structures and the organisation of prosecution agencies in the various jurisdictions of the United Kingdom. This chapter will explore different aspects pertinent to the various nations and will draw out some common overarching themes that have wider relevance.

The process of prosecution

In Chapter 2 we outlined that the criminal justice system can be viewed as a set of processes linking a range of agencies with separate but interrelated functions. Here we focus on the prosecution phase of this process, that is, the stage that begins with the police who, as the previous chapter has described, have a primary function of detecting and investigating crime. When a crime is reported or detected by the police, the police make an initial decision, based on the evidence available, whether to arrest and/or charge a suspect. Depending on the nature and circumstances of the offence (including the age of the alleged perpetrator), the police can decide on how to proceed with the case. The range of options available to the police is strictly prescribed by legislation and codes of practice, specifically the PACE (Police and Criminal Evidence Codes) applicable in England, Wales and Northern Ireland.[1]

Some of the options available to the police include issuing an informal warning or caution, or in some circumstances referring the case for a diversionary measure such as a restorative justice intervention (Sanders, 2002) (restorative justice approaches are discussed further in Chapter 8). If such *diversionary measures* are not appropriate, the police will pass the case (i.e. the file of evidence) to a separate prosecution service, who will assess the evidence and basing their decision on two main criteria – the evidential and public interest test – will decide how to proceed with the case. For the most part this involves whether or not to proceed to prosecute the case in the criminal courts, although in some circumstances prosecution services can also decide to divert a case from the courts. For example, in cases involving young people under the age of 18 in Northern Ireland, the Public Prosecution Service can make a decision to direct the case towards a diversionary restorative justice conference, rather than proceed to court (Doherty, 2010). In Scotland the Crown Office and Procurator Fiscal Service (COPFS) also has the authority to impose a direct measure such as a fine, and in such instances the case will not proceed to court.

As outlined in Chapter 2, in each of the jurisdictions of the United Kingdom prosecution services are separate from the police: the Crown Prosecution Service (England and Wales); the Public Prosecution Service (Northern Ireland); and the Crown Office and Procurator Fiscal Service (Scotland). The rationale for separating the policing and prosecution functions by having a separate body to assess the standard of evidence and make decisions on how to proceed with cases is illustrated in the following section, which describes the rationale and history of the establishment of the Crown Prosecution Service in England and Wales.

The history and development of the Crown Prosecution Service

Before the *Prosecution of Offences Act, 1879*, there was no public prosecutor to take criminal cases to court. People had to find their own lawyers or present the prosecution case themselves. Over time, as the criminal justice system became more formalised, the police began to play a important role in bringing prosecutions, and by the mid-1980s prosecutions were also brought by: the Director of Public Prosecutions (in cases of murder and a limited number of highly serious cases), Customs and Excise, the Inland Revenue and Local Authorities (Ashworth, 1998). However, difficulties with this prosecution system were highlighted in a range of arenas, and in 1978 a *Royal Commission on Criminal Procedure* was established to examine and report on the law and procedures governing the investigation and prosecution of crimes in England and Wales (Munday, 1981).

The Commission's report, published in 1981, made the following criticisms of the prosecution system in England and Wales:

- Differing procedures and standards were being applied about whether to prosecute or caution;
- The investigation and prosecution should be a separate process, and the police should not make the decision on whether to prosecute;
- The prosecuting lawyer should not have the officer who investigated the case as a client to be relied on to make a fair decision whether to prosecute;
- The police were allowing too many weak cases to come to court. This led to a high percentage of judge-directed acquittals;
- There was no accountability or control over the existing system.

(Royal Commission on Criminal Procedure
(Philips Commission) (1981))

The Commission recommended the establishment of a new independent prosecution authority, and a subsequent White Paper entitled *An Independent Prosecution Service for England and Wales (1983)* proposed the establishment of a *Crown Prosecution Service*. The *Prosecution of Offences Act, 1985* established the CPS and also specified a Code for Crown Prosecutors, which sets out its functions. The CPS has taken over the conduct of all criminal proceedings instituted by the police in England and Wales. Arguably the Commission's greatest impact was forming the basis for much of what later became the *Police and Criminal Evidence Act, 1984 (PACE)* (discussed in the previous chapter).

Following the enactment of the *Prosecution of Offences Act, 1985* the Crown Prosecution Service became operational in 1986. It represents a single independent and nationwide authority for England and Wales. It is independent of the police and has the power to discontinue prosecutions. Unlike prosecution agencies in other jurisdictions, it has no powers to institute proceedings or to direct the police to carry out any further investigations. Its introduction had substantial constitutional significance for a number of reasons. For the first time there was a single state prosecuting authority charged with making decisions of a quasi-juridical nature, which could ultimately affect the rights and liberties of the individual. It also created a new legal interest group directly linked to government. These lawyers, although civil servants, were expected to be independent of government control, but little was put in place to guarantee this, save the Code for Crown Prosecutors and existing Codes of Professional Conduct for Legal Professionals.

How is a prosecution decided?

The *Code for Crown Prosecutors* (2010a) is periodically updated (at the time of writing this book it is in its sixth edition) to reflect legislative and policy changes.[2] The Code is issued by the Director of Public Prosecutions under authority set out in the *Prosecution of Offences Act, 1985*. The Code sets out key principles and provides guidance to prosecutors on the general principles to be applied when making decisions about prosecutions. Alongside the Code, the CPS also publishes *Core Quality Standards* (2010b), which govern practice, but only the Code has the authority of law. The principle of independence from the police and other investigating agents is outlined in the Code:

> Although the prosecution service works closely with the police and other investigators, it is independent of them. The independence of prosecutors is of fundamental constitutional importance.
>
> *(Code for Crown Prosecutors*, 2010a: Section 1.5:2)

The Code further outlines the need for fairness, independence and objectivity to ensure equity in the administration of justice:

> Prosecutors must be fair, independent and objective. They must not let any personal views about the ethnic or national origin, gender, disability, age, religion or belief, political views, sexual orientation, or gender identity of the suspect, victim or any witness influence their decisions. Neither must prosecutors be affected by improper or undue pressure from any source. Prosecutors must always act in the interests of justice and not solely for the purpose of obtaining a conviction.
>
> *(Code for Crown Prosecutors*, 2010a: Section 2.4:3)

Further detail and guidance on the application of both the 'evidential' and 'public interest test' are provided in the Code. In the first instance prosecutors must assess if the evidence presented by the police or other investigators meets set criteria. Box 4.1 outlines how in considering the strength and quality of the evidence, the prosecutor must reflect on the following:

Box 4.1   Considering the evidence

Prosecutors must be satisfied that there is sufficient evidence to provide a realistic prospect of conviction against each suspect on each charge. They must consider what the defence case may be, and how it is likely to affect the prospects of conviction. A case which does not pass the

---

---

evidential stage must not proceed, no matter how serious or sensitive it may be.

A realistic prospect of conviction is an objective test based solely upon the prosecutor's assessment of the evidence and any information that he or she has about the defence that might be put forward by the suspect. It means that an objective, impartial and reasonable jury or bench of magistrates or judge hearing a case alone, properly directed and acting in accordance with the law, is more likely than not to convict the defendant of the charge alleged. This is a different test from the one that the criminal courts themselves must apply. A court may only convict if it is sure that the defendant is guilty.

(*Code for Crown Prosecutors*, 2010a: Sections 4.5 and 4.6: 7–8)

Notwithstanding the quality of the evidence the prosecutor must also consider if the evidence will be admissible in court. For example, there are legal rules governing the admissibility of evidence that must be considered. Bringing to mind the 'Confait Case' (see previous chapter), the Code specifically refers to evidence based on confession and asks the prosecutor to consider the following when assessing the admissibility and robustness of this evidence:

Is there evidence which might support or detract from the reliability of a confession? Is its reliability affected by factors such as the suspect's level of understanding?

(*Code for Crown Prosecutors*, 2010a: Section 4.7(e):9)

If evidential weaknesses are identified the prosecutor should seek to rectify these, for example, by requesting further information. However, if the evidential standard is ultimately not met, the prosecutor is obliged to stop the prosecution.

Following an assessment of the evidence, the second stage in determining whether a case will be brought further by the Crown Prosecution Service concerns an assessment of whether prosecution will be in the 'public interest'. Some of the factors more likely to lead to an assessment that prosecution is in the public interest include the commission of serious and harmful offences, and offences committed against public servants (e.g. members of the emergency services, public transport providers and prison officers). Conversely, if an offence is of a relatively minor nature where no harm was caused, this may tend against prosecution in the public interest. Furthermore, the prosecutor's code outlines that the prosecution service can consider if the defendant was suffering from significant mental and/or physical ill-health at the time of the commission of the offence in determining whether prosecution is in the public interest.

The question of 'public interest' assessments is one that, perhaps unsurprisingly, evokes attention from time to time. Cases involving 'assisted suicide', for example, have been the subject of public debate prompted in particular by Debbie Purdy, a woman with Progressive Multiple Sclerosis, who made an appeal on this issue to the House of Lords. This has led to the Director of Public Prosecutions, the head of the Crown Prosecution Service, issuing specific guidance in this area: *Policy for Prosecutors in Respect of Cases of Encouraging or Assisting Suicide (2010)*.[3]

Structure of the CPS

The Director of Public Prosecutions (DPP) is the national head of the Crown Prosecution Service. The DPP is appointed by and reports to the Attorney General, who is the Chief Legal Adviser to the Crown. The Crown Prosecution Service covers the whole of England and Wales, operating under a structure of 13 areas, with headquarters in London, Birmingham and York. It is the largest 'law firm' in the United Kingdom, and between April 2008 and March 2009 the CPS prosecuted 928,708 cases in the Magistrates' Courts and 103,890 cases in the Crown Courts (CPS, 2010c).

Northern Ireland

In Northern Ireland, the Public Prosecution Service (PPS), established in 2005 under provisions set out in the *Justice Act (Northern Ireland), 2002*, carries out broadly similar functions to the Crown Prosecution Service in England and Wales. The PPS takes decisions on cases brought by the police and is the principal prosecuting authority in Northern Ireland. The PPS is headed by the Director of Public Prosecutions for Northern Ireland, and is appointed by the Attorney General for Northern Ireland. The PPS is administratively divided into four regions covering the whole of Northern Ireland. In 2010–11 it dealt with a total of 58,821 cases (PPS, 2011). One of the ongoing issues in the Northern Ireland criminal justice system concerns 'avoidable delay', that is, delays in processing cases through the criminal justice system (Criminal Justice Inspection Northern Ireland, 2010). The PPS is part of an inter-agency project aiming to tackle the issue of delay in processing cases between the police and the prosecution services (Maguire, 2012).

Scotland

The Crown Office and Procurator Fiscal Service (COPFS) is responsible for the prosecution of crime in Scotland. This office also investigates suspicious deaths and complaints against the police. A Crown Agent and Chief Executive head the COPFS. The office covers the whole of Scotland and operates across three federations (North, West and East), a Procurator Fiscal heading each federation. Similar to the other jurisdictions, the COPFS operates independently of the police and considers cases presented by the police and other investigating agents before deciding what action to take in relation to the case. In common with other prosecution authorities, the evidence in the case and the public interest test inform decisions. Having considered these factors the Procurator Fiscal can decide what action is appropriate, including whether to prosecute the case, offer a direct measure (e.g. a fine) or to take no further action.

The options available to the Procurator Fiscal are set out in the COPFS' Code (2005). In most cases if there is sufficient evidence and prosecution is in the public interest the case will proceed to prosecution. The location of the prosecution (i.e. the level of the court) will be determined by the seriousness of the offence. In a variety of instances the Procurator Fiscal has a range of alternatives to prosecution, including taking no proceedings. The Procurator Fiscal also has the authority to issue a personal or written warning to the accused, advising that any repetition of alleged behaviour will be likely to result in a prosecution. Section 302 of the *Criminal Procedure (Scotland) Act, 1995* allows the Procurator Fiscal to make a conditional offer of a fixed penalty in respect of an offence of which an alleged offender could be tried in court. A range of penalties from £25 to £100 is available. Various diversionary measures are also available, for example, the Procurator Fiscal can refer the accused to a social worker, psychiatrist or a psychologist in lieu of prosecution (COPFS, 2001).

Despite significant organisational differences in the structure and administration of prosecution services across the various nations of the United Kingdom, there are a number of key common features. Firstly, the respective services provide expert legal scrutiny independently from the police (or other investigating agents) who assembled the evidence in the first instance. Secondly, in assessing the evidence two key tests are applied – the evidential and the public interest test. If the evidence meets these thresholds, and dependent on the circumstances of the case, the prosecuting bodies have a number of options available. In many cases this will involve proceeding to the next stage – prosecution in the courts.

Bail decisions

Another important aspect of the interaction between police, prosecutors and the courts involves decisions about bail. In England, Wales, Scotland and Northern Ireland, both **police** and the **courts** can attach conditions to bail. Police bail conditions are generally less restrictive than those that can be imposed by the court, and can include a requirement to report to the police station and to not contact certain persons (i.e. victims or witnesses). The courts can also impose conditions of curfew, a prohibition on entering certain areas and a requirement to reside at a specific address. In more recent years legislation has allowed the courts to impose a condition of an electronically monitored curfew (commonly referred to as a tag). There is evidence to suggest that the use of bail conditions has increased over time. Hucklesby (2009) makes the important point that bail conditions 'place restrictions on defendant's liberty when they are legally innocent so overuse or misuse of them should raise serious concerns' (Hucklesby, 2009: 11).

The imposition of conditions on bail or indeed the remand of a defendant in custody also signifies the fact that the police or courts consider the defendant to pose some sort of risk (e.g. the court may consider that the defendant presents a risk of absconding), and therefore some observers have argued that such decisions at the earlier stages of the criminal justice process can have knock-on effects on the ultimate outcome (Sanders & Young, 2007).

However, it is also important to note that a significant proportion of defendants who are made subject to bail conditions and/or remanded in custody may be ultimately found not guilty or acquitted. While time spent on remand in custody or subject to certain bail restrictions (e.g. electronic monitoring) can be deducted from an ultimate prison sentence, there is no recourse or recompense for defendants who are found not guilty or acquitted. This issue is thrown into particularly sharp relief when there are lengthy delays in the criminal justice process. Northern Ireland is a case in point. A review of the prison system in Northern Ireland conducted in 2011 highlighted that a significant number of the prison population were remand prisoners, some of whom had spent over 12 months on remand (Owers *et al.*, 2011).

The next section of this chapter explores the structure, administration and process of the courts.

Courts in the United Kingdom

Figure 4.1 provides an overview of the structures of the courts in England, Wales, Scotland and Northern Ireland. Despite differences in the organisation of the courts a number of common features apply. Firstly, a distinction can be made between criminal, civil and family law courts. Civil cases pertain to disputes between private individuals, for example, planning disputes. Family law cases concern childcare and custody issues, and can, for example, involve proceedings where social workers are proposing that a child be placed in the care of the state because of child protection and welfare concerns. Such proceedings are typically held *in camera* (i.e. in private), and the press is barred from identifying the names of the parties involved (Brayne & Carr, 2010.)

Criminal courts deal with cases brought as a result of criminal prosecutions, and these are the cases that we are concerned with here. A key principle of the justice system is that justice should 'be seen to be done', and as such criminal courts are generally open to the public and the proceedings can be reported on

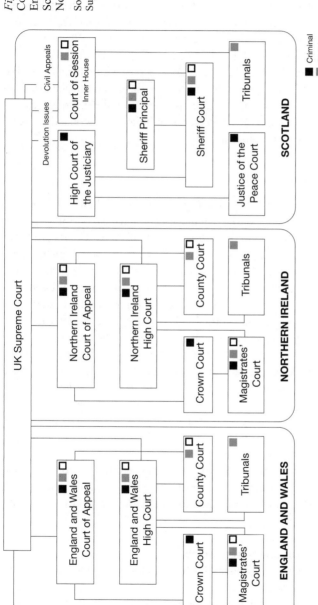

Figure 4.1
Court structures:
England, Wales,
Scotland and
Northern Ireland

Source: © UK
Supreme Court

in the press. There are some exceptions to this, most notably proceedings in the youth courts involving young people under the age of 18 (the different justice system for young people is discussed in Chapter 7).

The hierarchical nature of the court systems is another common feature. The lower courts (Magistrates' and Justice of the Peace Courts) hear and try less serious offences than the higher courts (Crown Court and Sheriff Court). Reflective of this, the lower courts have lesser sentencing powers. There are also mechanisms and processes of appeal within the courts system. Where a right of appeal is granted a higher court than that which made the original finding will hear this. The Supreme Court is the final court of appeal within the UK for **civil** cases; it hears cases involving public and constitutional importance affecting the whole of the United Kingdom. The Supreme Court also hears appeals in criminal cases for England, Wales and Northern Ireland. In Scotland the High Court of Justiciary hears criminal appeals.

Magistrates' Courts

Criminal cases begin in the Magistrates' Courts in England, Wales and Northern Ireland. Depending on the seriousness of the offence and the mode of trial a case can also be concluded in these courts. Cases in Magistrates' Courts are heard either by a panel of *Lay Magistrates* or a District Judge. Lay Magistrates are volunteers who are trained for the role, but they do not have formal legal qualifications. They sit as a panel of three to hear cases and are advised by a legally qualified clerk on matters of law and procedure. District Judges are qualified legal professionals who normally deal with more complex cases.

The concept of Lay Magistrates is intended to involve the community in the administration of justice, bringing 'common sense' and knowledge of 'ordinary life' to decision-making (Easton & Piper, 2008). Lay Magistrates were introduced in Northern Ireland following a *Review of the Criminal Justice System (Criminal Justice Review Group, 1999)*, which stemmed from the *Good Friday Peace Agreement*. The establishment of the role was provided in the *Justice (Northern Ireland) Act, 2002* and was recommended in order to foster stronger links between the courts and the community.

The question of how representative Lay Magistrates are of the local community is one that has been raised in studies on this area. For example, in a study of the Lay Magistracy in England and Wales, Morgan and Russell (2000) found that:

- 49 per cent of magistrates were women;
- only 4 per cent were aged under 40, whereas almost one-third (32 per cent) were aged 60 or over;
- although the ethnic origin of magistrates is approaching national representativeness, the make-up of benches varies markedly region by region;

- 40 per cent were retired, and 60 per cent identified their current or former occupation as professional or managerial.

Some offences are known as 'summary offences', which means that they can only be heard in the Magistrates' Court (for example, motoring offences or minor public order offences). The maximum penalty for a single summary offence is 6 months' imprisonment and/or a £5,000 fine (£2,000 in Northern Ireland). Magistrates' Courts also deal with more serious 'either way' offences, meaning offences that can be tried *either* in the Magistrates' or a Crown Court. The same maximum penalties apply.

For 'either way' offences the decision on whether the case will be held at a Magistrate or Crown Court level is determined by a number of factors. If a defendant pleads guilty to a triable 'either way' offence, the Magistrates' Court has the power to sentence, but the Magistrates may consider that a more severe penalty is required than is within their powers, and therefore the case can be sent to the Crown Court for sentencing. In such cases, lawyers acting for the prosecution services may make such an argument.

If a defendant pleads 'not guilty' to a triable either way offence, the Magistrates can send the case to the Crown Court for trial; the defendant can also request that the case be sent to the Crown Court for a trial. One of the major distinctions between the Magistrates' Court and the Crown Court is that trials in the latter are heard by a jury. Some cases are considered too serious to be heard in a Magistrates' Court – these are referred to as 'indictable only' offences. Examples of such offences include murder, rape and serious assaults.

Justice of the Peace Courts

Justice of the Peace Courts sit in Scotland. Similar to a Lay Magistrate, a Justice of the Peace is not legally qualified but sits with a legally qualified Clerk. The Clerk provides advice to Justices on legal and procedural matters.[4] Justice of the Peace Courts were created by the *Criminal Proceedings Etc. (Scotland) Act, 2007* (although the role of Justice of the Peace date back to the seventeenth century). They replace District Courts and allow more cases to be held at this level. The maximum penalty that a Justice of the Peace can impose is 60 days' imprisonment or a fine not exceeding £2,500. In Scotland there are two levels of criminal procedure: Solemn and Summary. Summary procedure involves less serious cases where there is a trial but no jury – this can take place at the Justice of the Peace Court and can be heard by a bench of three justices of the peace sitting together or a stipendiary magistrate. Summary procedures can also be heard in the Sheriff Court (the next level up from the Justice of the Peace Court). Solemn procedures are for the most serious cases and involve trial on indictment before a judge or a sheriff sitting with a jury.

Sheriff Courts

In Scotland the court above the Justice of the Peace Court is the Sheriff Courts. There are 49 Sheriff Courts in Scotland. Criminal cases under solemn procedures are heard by a Sheriff and a jury; cases under summary procedure (i.e. less serious offences) can be heard by a Sheriff alone. Sheriffs deal with the majority of criminal cases in Scotland, and there are currently 142 permanent Sheriffs. Permanent Sheriffs are legally qualified (with at least 10 years' experience) and are appointed by the Queen on the recommendation of the First Minister and the Judicial Appointments Board for Scotland. Unlike the Courts in England, Wales and Northern Ireland the accused in Scotland has no right to elect to be tried by a jury. Whether the matter is to be tried on a summary or solemn basis is decided by the prosecutor (MacPhail, 2006).

Crown Courts

The Crown Court is based at 77 centres across England and Wales, and normally sits in nine venues in Northern Ireland. It also hears appeals against decisions of Magistrates' Courts, and deals with cases sent for sentence from Magistrates' Courts. The Crown Court is presided over by a Circuit or a High Court Judge and a 12-person jury. Members of the public are selected for jury service or may have to go to court as witnesses. There are three levels of Crown Court centres:

1. First-tier centres, where both civil and criminal cases are tried and where the High Court Judge and Circuit Judge preside;
2. Second-tier centres, where High Court Judges or Circuit Judges preside but only deal with criminal cases; and
3. Third-tier centres, where Circuit Judges and Recorders deal with criminal cases, being mostly offences triable either way.

The types of criminal offence are divided into four classes, according to their gravity, and a High Court Judge can only try some, whereas Circuit Judges or Recorders can try others. Circuit Judges are full-time judges, although they may divide their time between civil and criminal work. Recorders and assistant recorders are part-time judges, whose main occupations are barristers, solicitors or (in a few instances) academics; most full-time judges start their judicial careers in this way. Appeals against sentence from the Crown Court go the Court of Appeal (Criminal Division). The appeal begins with the application being made on the behalf of the offender, which must be lodged with 28 days of the sentence. A single judge first considers the application. The single judge may grant leave for the case to proceed to the Court of Appeal, or he/she may refuse.

The Judiciary

Figures 4.2 and 4.3, based on data from England and Wales, illustrate that the judiciary is overwhelmingly male and white. In 2008, in terms of actual numbers, there were 94 male High Court Judges and 16 were women. If this figure is broken down in terms of ethnicity, one female and two males were drawn from a minority ethnic background. Out of the total of 94 male High Court Judges in 2008, 76 defined themselves as white. In 2008, the number of Circuit Judges reached a total of 566, but out of this total, only 87 were women. This number as a percentage represents 13, and in terms of ethnicity 2.5 per cent of the men are from an ethnic minority background compared to 77 per cent who defined themselves as white. Less than 1 per cent of females who are circuit judges are drawn from an ethnic minority background compared to 11 per cent who define themselves as white.

Juries

The principle of jury courts is that a person is tried in a forum of their peers. Jury courts operate in the higher courts in the UK and therefore deal with more serious offences. In England, Wales and Northern Ireland, juries are comprised of 12 members, while in Scotland juries comprise of 15 members. To be a member of a jury you must be over 18. The membership of the jury is drawn from the electoral register. Serving on a jury is considered to be a civic duty, and if summonsed you must serve unless there are reasonable grounds for not doing so (e.g. illness). There are some preclusions from jury membership,

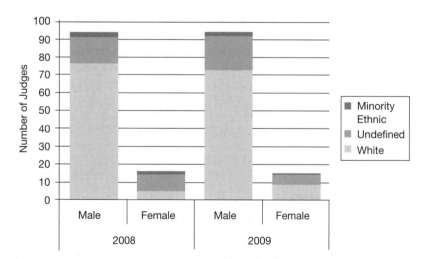

Figure 4.2 Ethnicity and gender of High Court Judges (England and Wales), 2008 and 2009

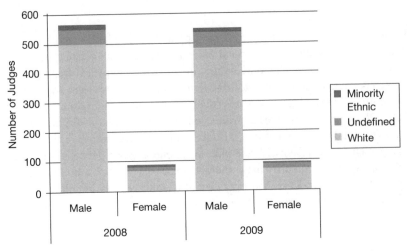

Figure 4.3 Ethnicity and gender of Circuit Court Judges in England and Wales, 2008 and 2009

including if you have served a prison sentence of more than five years. In specific cases you cannot serve on a jury if you know any of the parties involved in the alleged offence.

Jurors usually try the more serious criminal cases such as murder, rape, assault, burglary or fraud, and consequently only 5 per cent of cases might involve consideration by a jury. In England and Wales these trials take place in the Crown Court and, generally, the figure of 5 per cent is much lower as the majority of Crown Court cases involved a guilty plea and there is therefore no necessity for a jury to be sworn in. Each individual juror will be asked to consider the evidence presented and then decide whether the defendant is guilty or not guilty. Strict rules apply to the role of the juror. Once a trial has begun jury members are only allowed to discuss the case with fellow jury members in specified settings. Rules of confidentiality also pertain after the trial has ended – for example, it is considered contempt of court to discuss the deliberations of the jury. The parameters of jury confidentiality have been tested somewhat in recent years by the influence of social media (see Box 4.2).

Box 4.2   Tweeting jurors

The rise in the use of social media has caused problems in jury trials. Members of juries are legally prohibited from discussing the case outside of court and with anyone other than their fellow jury members. Perhaps most dramatically in Arkansas in the US, in 2011, a court decision of guilty in which the accused was sentenced to the death penalty was overturned because one of the jury members was found to have tweeted about the case during the trial.

In 2011, in England jury member Joanne Fraill was sentenced to eight months' imprisonment for contempt of court, after she contacted Jamie Sewart, one of the defendants in the case (who had been acquitted) on Facebook, the social networking site. Fraill discussed the case with Sewart, and because there were other defendants still on trial, the judge was obliged to discharge the jury and the case collapsed. Joanne Fraill admitted to revealing details of the jury's deliberations via conversation on Facebook, and also admitted to conducting her own research on the case on the Internet. She was prosecuted and convicted under the *Contempt of Court Act, 1981*.

When justice goes wrong

So far in this chapter we have outlined how the prosecution and court process is intended to work. There are some overarching principles that are supposed to govern the system, including that the criminal justice process should be fair, just and transparent. In theory all people should be treated equally before the law, and the outcomes of the criminal justice system should flow from these principles. We have, however, pointed towards some difficulties in the process, not least the question of representativeness in the administration of justice. One of the consistent criticisms made of the criminal justice system in the United Kingdom concerns differential treatment and outcomes.

In the UK concern with disproportionate representation or differential treatment of racial and ethnic minorities has been prominent since the mid-1980s. Numerous studies have found that certain minority ethnic groups are over-represented within the criminal justice system (Bowling & Phillips, 2002; Hood, 1992; Reiner, 2000). In part to address some of these concerns, in England and Wales, the *Criminal Justice Act, 1991*, introduced a legislative requirement to produce and publish statistics on an annual basis on the operation of the criminal justice system. This was, in the words of the Act, in order to 'avoid discriminating against any persons on the grounds of race or sex or any other improper ground' (*Criminal Justice Act, 1991*, Sect. 95, 1(b)).[5]

There are variations evident in the use of various sanctions throughout the criminal justice system that cannot be explained by the circumstances of the cases alone. There are several factors that determine these variations, such as discrimination on the basis of ethnicity (Bowling & Philips, 2002; Hood, 1992; Mhlanga, 1999), gender (Gelsthorpe & Morris, 2002; Hudson, 1998) and a variation in sentence decisions, which is dependent on the geography of the court and police decisions. This has been coined *'justice by geography'*, or in other words, the sentence you receive depends on which court you appear in rather than what you have done (Hucklesby, 1997). For example, in terms of ethnicity there is a wealth of research to show that some ethnic minority groups are overrepresented in the prison population, which is a cumulative effect of various factors that arise as people move through the criminal justice process (Hood, 1992). In terms of gender, it is widely known that women are treated differently to men in the criminal justice system. For example, Carlen (1983) and Hedderman and Gelsthorpe (1997) illustrate that some women are treated more leniently while others are treated more harshly.

There have been clear cases of miscarriages of justice that highlight how bias, discretion and discrimination can lead to variations in the type of sentences people receive. A 'miscarriage' means a failure to reach an intended destination or goal. A miscarriage of justice is, therefore, *mutatis mutandis*, a failure to attain the desired end-result of 'justice' (Rosenburg, 1992). A miscarriage occurs whenever suspects or defendants or convicts are treated by the State and are in breach of their rights, for one of six major reasons: first, because of deficient processes; second, because of the laws that are applied to them; third, because there is no factual justification for the applied treatment or punishment; fourth, whenever suspects or defendants or convicts are treated adversely by the State to a disproportionate extent in comparison with the need to protect the rights of others; fifth, whenever the rights of others are not effectively or proportionately protected or vindicated by State action against wrongdoers; or, sixth, by State law itself.

We do not intend to provide an in-depth discussion of the *causes célèbres* around which discussions about miscarriages of justice have taken place in the United Kingdom, but here are a few examples from recent times that will help to illustrate some of the categories listed in Box 4.3 and also to explain why reforms have occurred (Walker & Starmer, 1999). The analysis of such miscarriages has revealed no single cause but shows that different elements of the system itself have at times failed to provide *'justice for all'*.

Box 4.3   Miscarriages of justice

The so-called **Bridgewater Four** is the name given to four men convicted of killing 13-year-old paper-boy Carl Bridgewater, in Stourbridge, England in 1978. Michael Hickey, Vincent Hickey, James Robinson and Patrick Molloy were imprisoned in 1979. The convictions of the men mainly rested on the 'confession' of Patrick Molloy, which an appeal court later found was fabricated by the police. Patrick Molloy died in prison in

1981, and the surviving men were released in 1997. The appeal court quashed all of the convictions on the basis of 'tainted evidence'.

Colin Stagg was arrested and charged with the murder of Rachel Nickell on Wimbledon Common in 1992. Following his arrest Stagg was remanded to custody, and the evidence submitted to the court involved Stagg's own confession to the murder following a so-called 'honey-trap' (a set-up involving a female police officer).

In 1994 the case against Colin Stagg was thrown out after a judge ruled that it was inadmissible. There was no DNA evidence linking Stagg to the crime. In 2004 new DNA evidence showed that Robert Napper was linked to the offence. In 2008 Robert Napper was convicted of the manslaughter of Rachel Nickell, and the Metropolitan Police issued an apology to Colin Stagg.

The Birmingham Six were six Irish men convicted of pub-bombings, which killed 21 people in Birmingham in 1975. The six men – Paddy Hill, Hugh Callaghan, Richard McIlkenny, Gerry Hunter, Billy Power and Johnny Walker – were eventually released in 1991 having spent 16 years in prison as a result of a wrongful conviction. One of the most controversial aspects of the Birmingham Six case was the manner in which their appeals had been dealt with (Mullin, 1997).

Following this case the government established the Runciman Commission in 1993, which eventually led to the establishment of the Criminal Cases Review Commission (CCRC). The CCRC was set up in 1997 following the introduction of legislation (Criminal Appeal Act, 1995), and its purpose is to review miscarriages of justice in the criminal courts of England, Wales and Northern Ireland, and refer where necessary to courts of appeal. A similar Commission for Scotland, the Scottish Criminal Cases Review Commission, was established in 1999.

Latest data from the CCRC reveals the following:

Case statistics, figures to 31 March 2012

Total applications*:	*14,506*
Cases waiting:	247
Cases under review:	554
Completed:	13,969 (including ineligible), 498 referrals
Heard by Court of Appeal:	460 (321 quashed, 135 upheld, 4 reserved)

*Total applications includes 279 cases transferred from the Home Office when the Commission was set up in 1997.

Source: http://www.justice.gov.uk/about/criminal-cases-review-commission

These are some examples of reasons for miscarriages of justice: poor investigative procedures or oppressive interrogation practices used by the police; failure to disclose evidence by the prosecution; the trial court's failure to assess properly the weight of evidence; the unwillingness of the Appeal Court and the Home Office to admit that things had gone wrong (McConville *et al.*, 1994). A more recent case involving the wrongful conviction of a mother for the death of her two young sons is described in the case study at the end of this chapter.

Although this is not an exhaustive list of miscarriages of justice, we would like to highlight some of the cases that that have littered the criminal justice system over the last thirty years. These cases now form an essential part of the context of criminal justice reform, and it is important to include here a brief survey of the problems they brought to light. Miscarriages of justice expose some recurrent problems, including the concoction and falsification of evidence by the police officers and more generally non-disclosure by the prosecution to the defence.

Aside from the notorious cases, some indications should be given to the number of miscarriages produced overall. In a report in 1989, the organisation JUSTICE[6] estimated that up to 15 defendants a year sentenced for four years or more on indictment had been wrongly convicted. Just over 1 per cent of those convicted on indictment fall into this sentencing band, so the total number of miscarriages in the Crown Court may be well over 1,000 a year. As yet, no attempt has been made to estimate the rate in Magistrates' Courts, where over 90 per cent of cases are heard.

Conclusion

This chapter has introduced and explored the prosecution process by addressing the role of prosecution and courts across the various jurisdictions in the United Kingdom. The rationale for the separation of the prosecution function from the investigating agents, in this case the police, has been set out through a discussion on the history of the Crown Prosecution Service for England and Wales. It is notable that similar authorities exist across the UK jurisdictions applying similar principles to ascertain whether cases meet the criteria to proceed from case file to court. Other important decisions are taken in the passage of a criminal case from police to prosecution to court, including a decision on whether the defendant's liberty should be restricted pending the outcome of the court process. Remanding a defendant in custody is the most severe restriction that can be imposed, although a range of other restrictions known as 'bail conditions' can also be imposed.

The processing of a case through the court system is governed by strict rules. The criminal court system is hierarchical, and more serious cases are heard in higher courts where more severe penalties can be applied. Despite the strictures of law and rules and codes of practice governing various agencies within the system, miscarriages of justice do occur. This calls into question the impartiality of the law.

Glossary

Attorney General – is the Chief Legal Adviser to the Crown. The post-holder provides legal advice to the government.

Bail conditions – bail decisions can be made by the police and the courts pending the outcome of a prosecution. A number of conditions proscribed in law can be attached to bail. Examples include adherence to a curfew or a requirement to reside at a specific address.

Criminal Cases Review Commission (CCRC) – is an independent public body that was established under the *Criminal Appeal Act, 1995*. Its purpose is to review miscarriages of justice in the criminal justice system in England, Wales and Northern Ireland. The equivalent body dealing with cases in Scotland is the *Scottish Criminal Cases Review Commission.*

Justice by geography – is the term used to describe variations (when all other variables are the same) across geographical areas in decisions made by criminal justice agencies and institutions.

Case study

Sally Clark was wrongly convicted of the murder of her two baby sons in the 1990s, and spent more than three years in prison. Her first son died suddenly a few weeks after his birth in 1996, and when her second son died in the same manner in 1998 Clark was arrested and tried for murder. A central plank of the evidence used to convict Clark was given by the paediatrician, Professor Roy Meadows, who testified that the statistical likelihood of both deaths being as a result of sudden infant death syndrome (SIDS or cot-death) in the particular circumstances was highly improbable.

> It was explained to the jury that there were factors that were suggested as relevant to the chances of a SIDS death within a given family; namely the age of the mother, whether there was a smoker in the household and the absence of a wage earner in the family. None of these factors had relevance to the Clark family and Professor Meadows was asked if a figure of 1 in 8,543 reflected the risk of there being a single SIDS within such a family. He agreed that it was. A table from the CESDI report was placed before the jury. He was then asked if the report calculated the risk of two infants dying of SIDS

---

in that family by chance. His reply was: 'Yes, you have to multiply 1 in 8,543 times 1 in 8,543 and I think it gives that in the penultimate paragraph. It points out that it's approximately a chance of 1 in 73 million.'

(Extract from: Clark Appeal [2003] in the Supreme
Court of Judicature – Court of Appeal (Criminal Division)
[2003] EWCA Crim 1020)

The statistics on which Professor Meadows based his testimony were subsequently shown to be highly flawed. Meadows was struck off the General Medical Council register in 2005 and the Attorney General ordered a review of cases involving Meadows' testimony. At appeal it also emerged that the prosecution in this case had failed to disclose its own pathologist's microbiological reports, which suggested one of Clark's sons had died of natural causes. Sally Clark was released in 2003, but died of acute alcohol poisoning in 2007. In a statement following her death her family said: 'she never fully recovered from the effects of this appalling miscarriage of justice' (BBC, 7 September 2007).

Seminar questions

1. What factors should be taken into consideration when deciding whether a prosecution is in the 'public interest'?
2. Do you think being tried by a 'jury of your peers' is a fair system of justice?
3. Why do miscarriages of justice occur, and what does this say about the criminal justice process?

Further reading

Ashworth, A. & Redmayne, M. (2010) *The Criminal Process, 4th edn.* **Oxford: Oxford University Press**
This book provides a comprehensive guide to the criminal justice system and that of prosecution.

Sanders, A. & Young R. (2007) *Criminal Justice, 3rd edn.* **Oxford: Oxford University Press**
This book offers a critical analysis of the criminal justice system, how it operates, the stages involved in investigation, and processes, both pre- and post-trial.

Walker, C. & Starmer, K. (eds) (1999) *Miscarriages of Justice: A Review of Justice in Error.* **Oxford: Oxford University Press**

This book explores the criminal process and various aspects of miscarriages of justice in England and Wales. It contains detailed analysis of cases where justice has gone wrong.

Further information can be obtained from the following websites

The Attorney General's Office – http://www.attorneygeneral.gov.uk/

The Attorney General is the Chief Legal Adviser to the Crown. This website contains detailed information on the role and function of the Attorney General and includes a range of legal guidance.

The Crown Prosecution Service – http://cps.gov.uk

The website of the Crown Prosecution Service provides information on the service, including statistics on prosecutions across England and Wales. It also contains the *Code for Crown Prosecutors (2010)* and the Service's *Core Quality Standards*.

The Howard League for Penal Reform – http://www.howardleague.org/

The Howard League for Penal Reform is the oldest penal reform charity. The website provides a list of publications and case studies related to all aspects of the criminal justice system.

The Supreme Court – http://www.supremecourt.gov.uk/

The Supreme Court's website includes details on the court's procedures and the judgments of this court. Information is also provided on how to arrange a visit to the court.

References

Ashworth, A. (1998) *The Criminal Process: An Evaluative Study*, 2nd edn. Oxford: Oxford University Press

Bowling, B. & Phillips, C. (2002) *Racism, Crime and Justice*. Harlow: Longman

Brayne, A. & Carr, H. (2010) *Law for Social Workers*, 11th edn. Oxford: Oxford University Press

Carlen, P. (1983) *Criminal Women*. Oxford: Polity Press

Criminal Justice Inspection Northern Ireland (CJINI) (2010) *Avoidable Delay*. Belfast: CJINI

Criminal Justice Review Group (1999) *Review of the Criminal Justice System in Northern Ireland*. Belfast: Criminal Justice Review Group

Crown Office and Procurator Fiscal Service (2005) *Crown Office and Procurator Fiscal Service Prosecution Code*. Edinburgh: Crown Office

Crown Prosecution Service (2010a) *The Code for Crown Prosecutors*. London: CPS

Crown Prosecution Service (2010b) *Core Quality Standards*. London: CPS

Crown Prosecution Service (2010c) *Guide to the CPS*. London: CPS

Doherty, K. (2010) 'The development of restorative justice in Northern Ireland'. In W. Taylor, R. Earle & R. Hester (eds) *Youth Justice Handbook: Theory, Policy and Practice*. Cullompton: Willan Publishing, pp. 243–52

Easton, S. & Piper, C. (2008) *Sentencing and Punishment: The Quest for Justice*, 2nd edn. Oxford: Oxford University Press

Gelsthorpe, L. & Morris, A. (2002) 'Women's imprisonment in England and Wales', *Criminology and Criminal Justice*, 2, 3: 277–301

Hedderman, C. & Gelsthorpe, L. (1997) *Understanding the Sentencing of Women*, Home Office Research Study No. 170. London: Home Office

Her Majesty's Crown Prosecution Service Inspectorate (2001) *Report on the Thematic Review of the Quality of Prosecution Advocacy and Case Presentation*. London: HMCPSI

Her Majesty's Stationery Office (1983) *An Independent Prosecution Service for England and Wales*. White Paper. London: HMSO (Volume 9074 of Cmnd Series)

Hood, R. (1992) *Race and Sentencing*. Oxford: Oxford University Press

Hucklesby, A (1997) 'Court culture: An explanation of variations in the use of bail in magistrates' courts', *The Howard Journal*, 36, 2: 129–45

Hucklesby, A. (2009) 'Keeping the lid on the prison remand population: The experience in England and Wales', *Current Issues in Criminal Justice*, 21, 1: 3–23

Hudson, B. (1998) 'Doing justice to difference'. In A. Ashworth & M. Wasik (eds) *Fundamentals of Sentencing Theory*. Oxford: Clarendon Press, pp. 223–51

MacPhail, The Hon. Lord (2006) *MacPhail's Sheriff Court Practice*. Edinburgh: W. Green

McConville, M., Hodgson, J., Bridges, L. & Pavlovic, A. (1994) *Standing Accused: The Organization and Practices of Defence Lawyers in Britain*. Oxford: Clarendon Press

Maguire, M. (2012) 'Reducing avoidable delay'. Presentation to Agenda Northern Ireland Conference (2012). Available at: http://www.cjini.org/CJNI/files/09/09a229e1-5c63-484e-841e-674ff6b7a463.pdf [accessed on 3 June 2012]

Mhlanga, B. (1999) *Race and the Crown Prosecution Service*. London: The Stationery Office

Ministry of Justice (2011) *Statistics on Race and the Criminal Justice System 2010. A Ministry of Justice publication under Section 95 of the Criminal Justice Act 1991*. London: Ministry of Justice

Ministry of Justice Statistical Bulletin (2011) *Offender Management Statistics, Quarterly Bulletin, July to September 2010, England and Wales*

Morgan, R. & Russell, N. (2000) *The Judiciary in the Magistrates' Courts*. London: Home Office

Mullin, C. (1997) *Error of Judgement. The Truth About the Birmingham Bombings*. Dublin: Poolbeg Publications

Munday, R. (1981) 'The Royal Commission on Criminal Procedure', *The Cambridge Law Review*, 40, 3: 193–8

Owers, A., Leighton, P., McGrory, C., McNeill, F. & Wheatley, P. (2011) *Review of the Northern Ireland Prison Service*. Belfast: Prison Review Team

Philips, Sir C. (1981) *Royal Commission on Criminal Procedure (Philips Commission)*. London: HMSO

Public Prosecution Service (PPS) (2011) *Public Prosecution Service for Northern Ireland, Annual Report & Resource Accounts 2010–11*. Belfast: The Stationery Office

Reiner, R. (2000) *The Politics of the Police*, 3rd edn Oxford: Oxford University Press

Rosenburg, J. (1992) 'Miscarriages of justice'. In E. Stockdale and S. Casale (eds) *Criminal Justice Under Stress*. London: Blackstone, pp. 91–117

Runciman, V. (1993) *The Report of the Royal Commission on Criminal Justice.* Cm 2263. London: HMSO

Sanders, A. (2002) 'Prosecution systems'. In: M. McConville & G. Wilson (eds) *Handbook of Criminal Justice.* Oxford: Oxford University Press, pp. 149–67

Sanders, A. & Young, R. (2007) 'From sentence to trial'. In: M. Maguire, R. Morgan & R. Reiner (eds) *The Oxford Handbook of Criminology.* Oxford: Oxford University Press, pp. 953–90

Walker, C. & Starmer, K. (eds) (1999) *Miscarriages of Justice: A Review of Justice in Error.* Oxford: Oxford University Press

5 Probation and community justice

Key issues

- What is community-based punishment?
- How does the probation service and criminal justice social work 'protect the public'?
- What are the most effective means of encouraging people to stop offending?

Introduction

This chapter explores the context of community-based justice through the lens of current trends in probation practice. It begins by charting the development of probation practice in the late nineteenth century, noting that one of its founding rationales was offering an *alternative to custody*. The chapter proceeds to an analysis of current themes in practice. It documents the changed orientation of probation towards an agency whose primary articulated aim is *public protection*.

Alongside this reorientation there has been a marked expansion of the numbers of people who are being supervised by the probation service – both those sentenced to *punishment in the community* by the courts and released prisoners who are supervised by the probation service on licence. An increased emphasis on *enforcement* has meant that more and more people are being returned to custody for breaching their licences, and therefore probation and prison practice are mutually linked with what is described in the chapter as a *recycling effect*.

As in many areas of practice in the criminal justice system, the concept of 'risk' has become a core organising principle. This is evident in the process of *assessment*, the recommendations made to the courts and in the manner in which offenders are supervised in the community. Some of the implications of this risk-focused orientation are discussed and alternative approaches such as *desistance-focused practice* are explored.

Origins of probation

The origin of the probation service is traced back to 'court work missionaries' of the Victorian period (Nellis, 2004; Vanstone, 2004). These early volunteers are described as having a religious mission aimed at 'saving the souls' of those before the courts. Typically the court work missionary made an undertaking to work with a person who had appeared frequently before the courts to help them to desist from crime and thereby avoid further court appearances. Various historical accounts note that such work focused on temperance (encouraging abstention from alcohol) and welfare assistance (Fulton & Parkhill, 2009). In the context of the United Kingdom, the role was eventually formalised through the introduction of the *Probation of Offenders Act, 1907*, which set out the role of the 'Probation Officer' was to 'advise, assist and befriend' those placed under his or her supervision by the courts.

From welfare to public protection

A range of disposals introduced in various legislation expanded probation's role as an 'alternative to custody'. The types of community-based orders include:

- *Probation Order* – A specified period during which the offender must attend appointments with a probation officer and engage in activities as directed.
- *Community Service Order* – This order involves undertaking unpaid work in the community for a specified number of hours.

The core originating 'welfarist' principles remained key tenets of probation practice for much of the twentieth century. However, in parallel to developments elsewhere in the criminal justice system there has been a hardening of probation's focus. In the various jurisdictions of the United Kingdom there has been an evident shift in the discourse surrounding probation practice, with a repositioning of probation as a form of 'community punishment' as opposed to its previous incarnation as an 'alternative to punishment' (Brownlee, 1998).

Linked with these changes there has been a shift in probation's focus from 'advising, assisting and befriending' individuals towards an emphasis on 'protecting the public'. *Public protection* is variously conceived as a range of strategies employed to assess, manage and intervene to manage risk posed by individual *offenders*. Across numerous contexts, 'public protection' is situated as the top priority of probation practice, emphasising a shift in orientation away from probationers as clients towards the 'public' as the ultimate clients or consumers of the service (Smith & Vanstone, 2002).

Such changes, it is argued, are reflective of the increased punitiveness of criminal justice rhetoric and policies (Garland, 1985; 2001). This shift is visible in terminology within probation practice towards the routine use of the term 'offender' to describe clients of probation. Another has been the change in the requirements, for Probation Officers to be qualified social workers. For example, England and Wales introduced a separate training route for Probation Officers in the 1990s to reflect the shift in policy from a welfarist to a justice-oriented service (Burke, 2010; Knight & Ward, 2001). This picture is not universal, however, and Northern Ireland and Scotland retain the social work qualification for probation officers (Doran & Cooper, 2008), and probation practitioners in Scotland are called criminal justice social workers (McNeill, 2005).

Probation expansionism

One notable feature in all jurisdictions in the UK in recent years has been the increase of people who have been placed under the supervision of probation services. This increase could be viewed positively if it was matched by an associated reduction of the prison population, yet this is not the case. In roughly the same period that we witnessed an expansion of the prison population (from the late 1990s onwards) we also saw an expansion of community-based sentences. One of the obvious effects of this penal/probation expansionism is that larger numbers of people are under the gaze of criminal justice agencies, whether in the physical structure of the prison or under the supervision of the probation service.

Evidence of this expansionism in England and Wales is seen in the statistical data published by the Ministry of Justice. In 2009, the population under probation supervision was 241,500, representing an overall increase of 38 per cent in a ten-year period. In 1999, the total number under the supervision of the probation service was 109,700 (MoJ, 2010). This pattern, while different in scale, is also seen in the separate jurisdictions of Scotland and Northern Ireland.

Indeed, one of the main reasons for the increase in probation caseloads in this period is linked to the rise in the prison population. The Probation Service has traditionally supervised people leaving custody on licence. This means that if a person was to be sentenced to ten years in prison, they could be released 'on licence' eight years into their sentence. Being released 'on licence' means that there are conditions attached to a person's release, such as a specification on where they should live and a requirement that they do not engage in any further criminal activity. For prisoners on longer sentences the period spent 'on licence' also meant being supervised by a Probation Officer, so a released prisoner may have to attend a weekly meeting at a probation office and to gain support in accessing education or employment. Failing to adhere to the terms of a licence constitutes a *breach*, and in these circumstances a released prisoner can be returned to prison (referred to as *recall*) for a specified period of time.

Previously post-custody supervision by the probation service was reserved for those prisoners serving longer sentences. However, the introduction of new legislation into England and Wales – the *Criminal Justice Act, 2003* – has meant that many more sentenced prisoners are subject to some form of post-custody supervision by the probation service following their release from prison (Padfield & Maruna, 2006). One of the net effects of these greater numbers is that more people are breaching the terms of their licences and are being returned to prison. One can therefore say that there is a *recycling effect* produced by this increased penal/probation gaze, meaning that a large proportion of individuals are being *recycled* through the prison and probation system and back into prison again.

Statistics published by the Ministry of Justice record that in 2009–10 in England and Wales 13,900 offenders subject to *determinate custodial sentences* were recalled to prison for breaching the terms of their licence. This represented an increase of 18 per cent from the previous year (2008–9) (MoJ, 2010). This *recycling effect* is therefore a significant contributor to the high prison population in England and Wales. Figure 5.1 provides an illustration of the parallel increase in probation and prison numbers since 1999.

In addition to the legislative and administrative changes that have been responsible for this penal/probation expansionism there has been increased pressure on the probation service to demonstrate that it is effective in its stated purpose of *public protection.*

Public protection, risk and probation

As Robinson and McNeill (2004) note, *public protection* has become something of a meta-narrative for probation. While protecting the public can on one hand appear like an eminently laudable aim, on the other hand it is a nebulous and essentially unrealisable concept – how exactly does one protect the public? Here the promise of public protection can be linked to the ascendancy of risk as a central orienting principle.

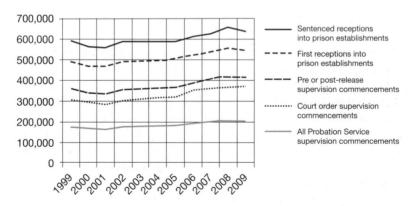

Figure 5.1 Probation and prison populations, 1999–2009

Source: Ministry for Justice (2010): 7

The orthodoxy of risk

The concept of *risk* has become a central organising principle of the criminal justice system. What does this mean? In an important contribution to criminological literature, Feeley and Simon (1994) coined the term *actuarial justice* to refer to the manner in which criminal justice policies and systems had adopted and adapted techniques more ordinarily associated with the insurance industry to calculate levels of *risk* and to implement measures to 'manage these risks'.

The practice of *risk assessment* can be characterised as one such technique. In probation practice assessment of risk generally covers two main domains – *risk of reoffending and risk of harm*. Risk of reoffending refers to the likelihood or otherwise of an individual committing further offences, while risk of harm refers to the potential of such behaviour to cause harm. The two domains of risk are not necessarily always connected. For example, someone who commits shoplifting offences to fund drug use may be assessed as posing a high risk of reoffending – that is, they are highly likely to do this in the future – but such offences present a low risk of harm – that is, there is little chance of someone being physically harmed by this behaviour. However, someone who commits a one-off murder may present a low risk of reoffending but a high risk of serious harm *if* they were to reoffend.

A range of risk assessment tools and frameworks combining *actuarial* and *clinical* measures of assessment has been developed for use in probation practice. An actuarial assessment of risk is a statistically derived measure based on a range of factors, such as age at first conviction. A clinical assessment of risk is based on the practitioner's assessment, typically derived from interviewing, observation, professional judgement and knowledge (Beech *et al.*, 2003; Kemshall, 2003).

Probation officers (and prison staff) in England and Wales use the *OASys (Offender Assessment System)*[1] tool to assess the offender under the following headings:

1. Accommodation
2. Education, training and employability
3. Financial management and income
4. Relationships
5. Lifestyle and associates
6. Drug misuse
7. Alcohol misuse
8. Emotional well-being
9. Thinking and behaviour
10. Attitudes
11. Health and other considerations

For each section the probation officer is required to score how each of these areas may contribute to further offending and to therefore arrive at an overall assessment of risk of reoffending. Similarly, the risk of harm is gauged by assessing factors such as previous harm caused, the seriousness of the current offence(s), whether there is a known victim and whether the person has used or is likely to use weapons.

The analysis of what constitutes a risk of offending is based on research on *risk factors*, a large body of work exploring the relationships between a range of variables and offending (e.g. Andrews *et al.*, 2006; Farrington, 1994; 2007). Typically risk assessment tools such as *OASys* include an analysis of *dynamic* and *static* risk factors. A static risk factor is something that cannot be changed, such as age at first conviction, whereas a dynamic risk factor is something that can change – drug use is one example.

All of this may sound eminently plausible – you might ask what is wrong with looking at this range of factors and based on this assessing whether someone is likely to commit a further offence and/or cause serious harm? Well, firstly, risk assessment is not an exact science, and nor, to be fair, does it necessarily claim to be. The problem is, however, that it is sometimes portrayed as such. This feeds the illusion that we can somehow predict the future and control and punish people based on the possibilities of their future behaviour. Carlen (2008) has referred to this as the 'imaginary' of 'risk-crazed governance'.

Secondly, the attribution of risk has become the means through which resources are allocated. In other words, the higher the assessed risk the more intensive the intervention. Again, fair enough, you might say, but viewing individuals as a conglomeration of risks to be managed does not necessarily address the reasons for offending, and nor does it address why someone should be motivated to change.

Risk, need and responsivity

The question of what probation does with people in order to reduce risk or what is *effective practice* has become central to practice in recent years. One of the key tenets of *effective practice* set out in a range of literature is that interventions should be targeted at the level of risk posed. In the simplest terms, the higher the assessed risk of reoffending and risk of harm, the greater the level of intervention required. This principle is illustrated in Figure 5.2 in what the *National Offender Management Service* terms the 'Tiered Model of Offender Management'. Here we see that the higher-tiered offender (higher risk) receives a more intensive intervention.

This framework is consistent with the *Risk–Need–Responsivity (RNR)* model of offender rehabilitation (Ward & Maruna, 2007). The *RNR Model* (for short) argues that interventions with offenders should be based on the level of risk and targeted towards *criminogenic need*. The term *criminogenic need* refers to

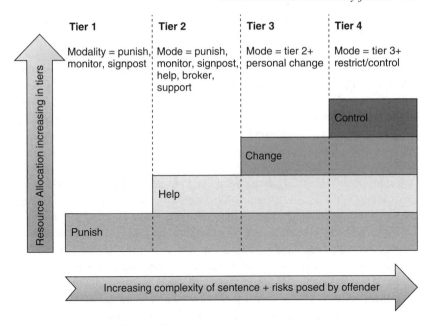

Figure 5.2 'Tiered model of offender management'

Source: Adapted from *The NOMS Offender Management Model* (London: National Offender Management Service, 2005): 17

those factors (the risk factors described earlier) that are assessed as being associated with offending. So, for instance, alcohol misuse may be a *criminogenic need* if it is linked to a person's offending, such as when a person becomes threatening and abusive and commits assaults when drunk. The *responsivity* component of the model refers the need to target interventions aimed at addressing offending behaviour towards the individual's learning style.

This model of offender rehabilitation has become the orthodoxy of probation practice in recent years, linked to initiatives that have sought to demonstrate probation's effectiveness in reducing recidivism (reoffending). In particular the '*What Works*' initiative launched in England and Wales by the Home Office in the 1990s, was based on a range of research evidence demonstrating the effectiveness of certain approaches, specifically cognitive-behavioural group work programmes, in reducing offending, which led to wide-scale investment in these particular methodologies and approaches (Merrington & Stanley, 2004).

Cognitive-behavioural approaches explore the way in which thoughts (cognition) and feelings (emotion) interact with behaviour. The central premise of cognitive-behavioural interventions is that aspects of cognition, including what are termed negative thought patterns or maladaptive problem-solving skills, influence affect (feelings) and, therefore, behaviour (McGuire, 2005). Some of the literature on effective practice has found that delivering cognitive-behavioural programmes in group-work settings produced positive results, that is, a reduction in levels of reoffending (Lipsey *et al.*, 2007).

The delivery of offending-behaviour programmes based on these broad underlying principles has become a core business of probation. There is a range of *accredited programmes* delivered by probation personnel, in which offenders can be required to partake as a condition of their sentence. Similarly, in prisons offending-behaviour programmes (often run by probation staff) have become (in theory at least) a core component of prison sentences, with prisoners being required to complete specific programmes in order to be considered for parole (early conditional release).[2]

Examples of offending behaviour programmes include the *Think First* programme, which targets 'general offending', typically involving offences such as theft, burglary, damage to property and driving offences. *Think First* focuses on areas such as consequences of offending, tackling pressure to offend, problem-solving, self-control and goals and strategies for the future. The programme is delivered over four pre-group sessions, 22 group work sessions (each last approximately two hours), followed by seven individual post-group sessions (McGuire, 2005). To put this into perspective, the amount of time that a person is required to attend a programme is longer than the typical academic module.

Indeed, one of the difficulties of programme delivery is the problem of attrition, or people failing to complete programmes for a variety of reasons. This situation can lead to a person being in breach of their order and being returned to court with the possibility of receiving a custodial sentence or being returned to custody. This perpetuates the *recycling effect* that was referred to earlier in this chapter. See Box 5.1 for some examples of offending behaviour programmes.

Box 5.1   Other examples of offending behaviour programmes delivered by probation in various areas

- Integrated Domestic Abuse Programme (IDAP)
- Community Domestic Violence Programme (CDVP)
- Healthy Relationships Programme [delivered in custody]
- Thames Valley Sex Offender Group Work Programme (TVSOGP)
- Northumbria Sex Offenders Groupwork Programme
- Drink Impaired Drivers
- Addressing Substance Related Offending
- Aggression Replacement Training
- Steer Clear (Drink-Drive Programme)

Managing offenders and protecting the public

Alongside the increased risk-focused nature of probation practice there has also been a hardening of the functions of probation. No longer conceived as an 'alternative to punishment', probation is now firmly situated as an agency that *delivers* punishment. This hardening of its functions has largely arisen as a result of the external political climate in which the probation service has been shuffled about between the rocks of prison and punitive populism. The establishment of the *National Offender Management Service (NOMS)* in England and Wales in 2004 further linked the functions of probation and the prison service. NOMS is an executive agency of the Ministry of Justice, which brings together the headquarters of the Probation Service and HM Prison Service. The service is responsible for the commissioning and delivery of 'offender management services' across England and Wales. While the Probation Service comprises of 35 probation trusts, it receives its funding from NOMS, to which it is accountable for performance and service delivery.

The stated rationale of NOMS, as the name suggests, is of 'offender management'. The *Correctional Services Review (2003) [Carter Report]* identified that the prison and probation services did not work in a sufficiently 'joined-up' way to reduce offending, and recommended that 'a more strategic approach to the end-to-end management of offenders across their sentence is needed' (Correctional Services Review, 2003: 23).

The concept of offender management was introduced. Offender management, according to NOMS, has different meanings. It refers to the 'high-level and interlocking structures and processes' through which the whole population of offenders is managed, and it also refers to management of the individual offender across the course of their sentence. Critics of NOMS have argued that its establishment has led to a further erosion of the probation service's identity and is representative of a 'punitive managerial' rationale (Gregory, 2010: 2274).

Figure 5.3 represents the NOMS' conceptualisation of the 'offender's journey through the system'. The route on the right represents the prison stage of the offender's journey, the left-hand route the probation phase. Taken as a whole it highlights the conceptual interconnectedness of prison and probation.

Jurisdictional differences

Throughout this chapter attention has been focused on the probation service in England and Wales. It is important to note, however, that there are distinct differences in how probation is organised and practised elsewhere in the United Kingdom. In Scotland, for example, the Probation Service was disbanded in 1969 and criminal justice social workers were established as practitioners within local authority social work departments (McNeill, 2005). Scotland remains distinct in the fact that the responsibility for the assessment, supervision and

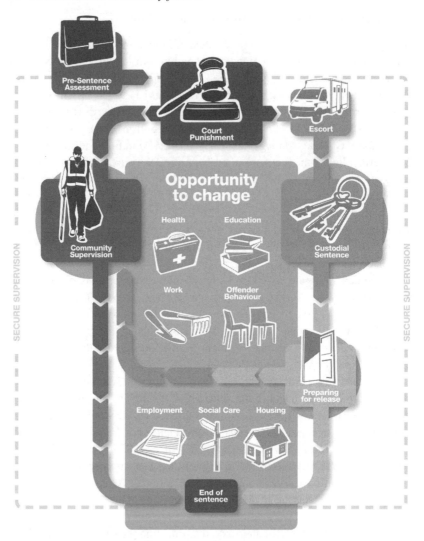

Figure 5.3 'The offender's journey through the system'

Source: NOMS Offender Journey Map http://www.justice.gov.uk/downloads/about/noms/noms-offender-journey-map.pdf

monitoring of offenders remains the responsibility of local authorities (as distinct from a separate probation service).

More recently, the introduction of the *Management of Offenders (Scotland) Act, 2005* led to the establishment of eight 'Community Justice Authorities'. The role is to reduce reoffending through the coordination of the work of criminal justice agencies (e.g. police, criminal justice social work, prisons). These authorities have been operational since 2007. A further distinct focus of criminal justice social work in Scotland has been the re-emergent focus on *reparation* (or pay-back to the community for the harm caused by crime) as opposed to an emphasis on punishment (McNeill, 2011).

In Northern Ireland, the Probation Board for Northern Ireland (PBNI) was established following the introduction of legislation in 1982.[3] The Board comprises of representatives from the local community and it oversees the operation of the service, which employs approximately 300 probation staff. Importantly, in Northern Ireland the development and structure of the probation service (as with other agencies in the criminal justice system) has been influenced by the context of the *Troubles*. As a result of this particular context the probation service in Northern Ireland was required to develop innovative responses, and as such it has traditionally occupied a more community-based role, working with local agencies to deliver services (Chapman & O'Mahony, 2007).

However, despite the very different organisational structures under which probation operates in the various parts of the United Kingdom, the trends of an increased focus on risk, an emphasis on 'effective practice' – generally interpreted as meaning the RNR model – and an overriding concern with public protection can be seen across the different jurisdictions (Chapman & O'Mahony, 2007; Robinson & McNeill, 2004).

Hostages to fortune?

The question of whether probation can or should be an agency in which public protection is the overarching priority is one that McNeill and Weaver debate:

> To talk of public protection seems to make sense in times of insecurity; probation's political position and its claims on public resources may seem to be best legitimated by promising to manage and reduce risks and thus to enhance security. However, whenever offender management commits itself to assessment and management of risks, it exposes itself not to the likelihood of failure, but to its inevitability. Not all risks are predictable and not all harms are preventable. Even being excellent at assessing and managing risks most of the time – assuming that this could be achieved – would not protect probation from occasional, spectacular failures and the political costs that they carry.
>
> (McNeill & Weaver, 2010: 11)

The perceived (and inevitable) 'failure' of the probation service to adequately fulfil its public protection function was seen in the high-profile 'Sonnex' case in London in 2008, when Dano Sonnex, a person who was subject to probation supervision, committed two murders (see case study at the end of this chapter).

While there has been an increased emphasis on risk management that is premised on a knowledge base that has explored the factors relating to offending, the following section of this chapter explores the concept of desistance – that is, the reasons why people cease to offend.

What is desistance?

An emphasis on risk management and public protection is a core feature of current probation practice, manifest in the assessment of and engagement with people who have committed crime. Nonetheless, there are other discourses of rehabilitation that have gained increasing prominence. These focus on the reasons why people may be motivated to stop or *desist from offending*. At its simplest *desistance* refers to the processes through which people cease offending. Broadly speaking, research has focused on three main aspects of desistance (Maruna, 2000):

- Maturational reform (growing out of crime)
- Social bonds
- Narrative

The concept of *maturational reform* draws on a wide range of literature that examines the links between age and offending, and demonstrates that most people simply 'grow out of crime'. Criminal justice data consistently demonstrates that the majority of known offending is committed by young men, primarily adolescents and adults in their twenties (Smith, 2007). The age/crime curve presents strong evidence that the processes of ageing and maturation have an impact on desistance from offending. However, as several desistance theorists argue, maturation or ageing is just one (albeit very important) part of the process of desistance.

The second major strand of desistance literature has explored the importance of social bonds in supporting a cessation from offending. Drawing on *social control theories* (Hirschi, 1969), this literature argues that people with stronger positive social bonds are more likely to desist from offending for a variety of reasons, including the fact that they may ultimately have 'more to lose'. Social Control Theory broadly conceived argues that people's relationships, social norms, beliefs and values are important factors in whether people break the law. Hirschi (1969) argued that stronger social controls meant that offending was less likely.

Key life transitions such as entering into a committed partnership or attaining employment can be seen as strengthening social bonds and therefore encouraging a cessation from offending (Laub *et al.*, 1998). Of course, it is important to note that the quality of these bonds is an important variable –being in an abusive relationship is not going to aid desistance, and in fact is likely to have the opposite effect.

In recognition of the fact that pathways to desistance are variable – the factors that lead one person to stop offending may be considerably different for another person – the importance of *narrative* in the process of desistance has been explored (Farrall & Bowling, 1999; Maruna, 2001; Vaughan, 2007). Here the importance of the subjective perspectives of individuals in their accounts of desistance is noted. How people view themselves and make sense of their past experiences and future aspirations is an important aspect of ceasing to offend. This can involve a shift from viewing oneself as an offender – someone who commits crime – to a person who has other attributes and is not necessarily defined by this label.

Here the importance of establishing alternative narratives is important in terms of making the shift from offender to non-offender. A sense of 'self-effi-cacy' is important in the process of desistance (Maruna, 2001). What this means is that desistance can occur where a person perceives himself or herself as having a sense of agency or a sense of being in control of his own life – that is, the opposite of thinking 'shit happens'. Burnett and Maruna (2004) also note the importance of 'hope', which can be linked to a person's general outlook and disposition. Being able to pay back or make amends, referred to in the litera-ture as *generativity*, is also seen as important in people's journeys, to borrow Maruna's (2001) phrase, towards *'making good'*.

Importantly, however, as McNeill and Weaver (2010) note in a review of the literature in this area, there are key interdependencies between individual circumstances and structural factors. For example, feelings of hope, self-efficacy and motivation to change cannot be disaggregated from the environment and circumstances in which people live. In other words, there is a need to address aspects of *social* and *human capital* (Farrall, 2002; 2004).

Desistance-based practice

Drawing on the findings of the burgeoning literature on desistance, increasing attention has been paid to promoting desistance through probation practice (e.g. Burnett, 2004; Burnett & McNeill, 2005; McNeill & Weaver, 2010). In some senses this has presented challenges to the existing orthodoxy of the *risk–need–responsivity* model of practice. For one thing it involves changing the lens through which 'offenders' are viewed, and indeed if the literature on the importance of narratives and identity change is to be taken seriously, this would involve the abandonment of such profoundly labelling terms as 'offender' in the first instance.

Viewed through the dystopic RNR lens, 'offenders' are regarded as risk entities to be measured and managed within an overarching rubric of public protection. Implicit in such a view is that 'offenders' are outside the 'public' for whom protection is afforded. Secondly, viewing people as risk subjects may speak to how they may be managed (effectively or otherwise) but it does not necessarily speak to how people themselves may be motivated to change (Ward & Maruna, 2007).

Conclusion

This chapter has briefly set out the original 'welfarist' orientation of the probation service and has noted the change in direction from the purpose of probation as an 'alternative to custody' towards a form of 'punishment in the community'. The extent of the expansion of the population under the supervision of the probation service has been set out, as has the parallel and interrelated rise in the custodial population. The probation services' aim of 'protecting the public' through the management of risk has been critically explored, and alternative paradigms such as 'desistance-based practice' have been described.

While arguments in support of a desistance-based paradigm for probation practice (McNeill, 2006) are likely to find a receptive audience among probation practitioners who have some affinity to the original probation ethos of 'advising, assisting and befriending', key questions regarding how probation works to increase the *social capital* of individuals on probation within an overarching orthodoxy of risk and public protection remain.

Glossary

Criminogenic need – A factor associated with offending.

National Offender Management Service (NOMS) – An executive agency of the Ministry of Justice, which coordinates the directorates of the Probation Service and Prison Service in England and Wales.

Pre-sentence Report (PSR) – A report on the offender requested by the court following conviction and prior to sentencing. The report typically includes an analysis of the offence or offences and a section on the offender's background and living circumstances. It includes an assessment of risk of reoffending and risk of harm, and it concludes by making a recommendation to the court regarding sentencing.

RNR Model – This refers to the 'Risk–Need–Responsivity' Model of offender rehabilitation, in which the level of intervention is targeted towards the assessed level of risk and *criminogenic need*. The responsivity component refers to adapting the intervention to suit the offender's learning style.

Case study

The Sonnex Case

The 'Sonnex Case' refers to the torture and murder of two French students, Laurent Bonomo and Gabriel Ferez, in New Cross, London in June 2008 by Dano Sonnex and Nigel Farmer. At the time of these killings Dano Sonnex was subject to probation supervision on a post-release licence from custody. Sonnex had originally been sentenced to eight years' imprisonment in March 2003 at the age of 17 for offences of assault with intent to resist arrest, having an imitation firearm with intent, attempted robbery, robbery x 4 and wounding with intent.

When Bonomo and Ferez were murdered in 2008 there was an outstanding arrest warrant for Sonnex's recall to prison because he had breached his licence condition by being charged with a further offence of 'handling stolen goods'. Before the recall was affected Sonnex and Farmer committed the brutal murders, breaking into the flat of the French students and binding both Bonomo and Ferez by their hands and feet, and subjecting them to a prolonged torture that resulted in their deaths.

Subsequent investigations into the case highlighted shortcomings in the probation service's risk assessment and delays in processing Sonnex's recall to prison. High probation caseloads and staff shortages were noted as contributory factors. Sonnex's supervising probation officer had a caseload of 127 people and was qualified for just one year (Morgan, 2009). As a result of the shortcomings in this case, the Chief Probation Officer in the London Probation Area resigned.

One of the outcomes of the review of this case was increased pressure to recall to prison people who had breached their licence in any way.

Seminar questions

1. Considering the Sonnex Case, is the stated aim of the probation service to 'protect the public' a reasonable and feasible objective?
2. What are some of the possible reasons for the increase in the numbers of people being placed under the supervision of probation services?
3. What are some of the benefits and shortcomings of the *'Risk–Need–Responsivity'* Model of rehabilitation?

Further reading

McNeill, F. & Weaver, B. (2010) *Changing Lives? Desistance Research and Offender Management.* **Glasgow: The Scottish Centre for Crime and Justice Research**
This publication provides an overview of some of the key literature on desistance and offers guidance on how desistance can be supported in practice.

Priestly, P. & Vanstone, M. (2010) *Offenders or Citizens? Readings in Rehabilitation.* **Cullompton: Willan Publishing**
This book, an edited collection of some key readings on the concept of rehabilitation and the role of probation services in this area, provides an excellent entry into some key issues and debates in this area.

Ward, T. & Maruna, S. (2007) *Rehabilitation: Beyond the Risk-Paradigm.* **London: Routledge**
Part of the 'Key Readings in Criminology' series, this book presents an excellent introduction into the evidence base for models of intervention and provides a persuasive critique of the RNR model.

Further information can be obtained from the following websites

Further information on desistance from crime, include links to a range of literature and an insightful documentary on this topic can be accessed from this site: http://blogs.iriss.org.uk/discoveringdesistance/

This website provides some fictionalised scenarios of probation cases and asks you to decide how the court should deal with these by formulating a sentence recommendation: http://www.directgov.coionline.tv/judgeforyourself/

The website of the Probation Board for Northern Ireland contains information on the structure and operation of probation in Northern Ireland. It also provides free access to the *Irish Probation Journal*, which contains a range of articles on probation: www.pbni.org.uk/

References

Andrews, D.A., Bonta, J. & Wormith, J.S. (2006) 'The recent past and near futures of risk and/or need assessment', *Crime and Delinquency*, 52, 1: 7–27
Beech, A.R., Fisher, D.D. & Thornton, D. (2003) 'Risk assessment of sex offenders', *Professional Psychology: Research and Practice*, 34, 4: 339–52
Brownlee, I. (1998) *Community Punishment: A Critical Introduction.* London: Longman
Burke, L. (2010) 'Probation qualifications framework: Getting the right balance', *Probation Journal*, 57, 1: 3–8
Burnett, R. (2004) 'One-to-one ways of promoting desistance: In search of an evidence-base'. In: R. Burnett and C. Roberts (eds) *What Works in Probation and Youth Justice.* Cullompton: Willan Publishing, pp. 180–97

Burnett, R. & Maruna, S. (2004) So 'prison works', does it? The criminal careers of 130 men released from prison under Home Secretary Michael Howard', *Howard Journal of Criminal Justice*, 43, 4: 390–404.

Burnett, R. & McNeill, F. (2005) 'The place of the officer–offender relationship in assisting offenders to desist from crime', *Probation Journal*, 52, 3: 247–68

Carlen, P. (2008) (ed.) *Imaginary Penalities*. Cullompton: Willan Publishing

Carter, P. (2003) *Managing Offenders, Reducing Crime. A New Approach*. London: Home Office

Chapman, T. & O'Mahony, D. (2007) 'Youth and criminal justice in Northern Ireland'. In: G. McIvor & P. Raynor (eds) *Developments in Social Work with Offenders*. London: Jessica Kingsley Publishers, pp. 99–113

Doran, P. & Cooper, L. (2008) 'Social work: The core qualification of probation officers in Northern Ireland', *Irish Probation Journal*, 5: 23–35

Farrall, S. & Bowling, B. (1999) 'Structuration, human development and desistance from crime', *British Journal of Criminology*, 39, 2: 253–68

Farrington, D. (1994) 'Human development and criminal careers'. In M. Maguire, R. Morgan & R. Reiner (eds) *The Oxford Handbook of Criminology*. Oxford: Oxford University Press, pp. 511–84

Farrington, D. (2007) 'Childhood risk factors and risk-focussed prevention'. In M. Maguire, R. Morgan & R. Reiner (eds) *The Oxford Handbook of Criminology*, 4th edn. Oxford: Oxford University Press, pp. 602–40

Feeley, M. & Simon, J. (1994) 'Actuarial justice: The emerging new criminal law'. In D. Nelken (ed.) *The Futures of Criminology*. London: Sage, pp.173–201

Fulton, B. & Parkhill, T. (2009) *Making the Difference: An Oral History of Probation in Northern Ireland*. Belfast: Probation Board for Northern Ireland

Garland, D. (1985) *Punishment and Welfare: A History of Penal Strategies*. Aldershot: Gower

Garland, D. (2001) *The Culture of Control*. Oxford: Oxford University Press

Gregory, M. (2010) 'Reflection and resistance: Probation practice and the ethic of care', *British Journal of Social Work*, 40, 7: 2274–90

Hill, L. (2009) *Investigation into the Issues Arising from the Serious Further Offence Review. Dano Sonnex [DS] (d.o.b. 07.07.85, age 23)*. London: National Offender Management Service

Hirschi, T. (1969) *Causes of Delinquency*. Berkeley: University of California Press

Kemshall, H. (2003) *Understanding Risk in Criminal Justice*. Buckingham: McGraw-Hill/Open University Press

Knight, C. & Ward, D. (2001) 'Qualifying probation training: Implications for social work education', *Social Work Education*, 20, 2: 176–86

Laub, J.H., Nagin, D.S. & Sampson, R.J. (1998) 'Trajectories of change in criminal offending: Good marriages and the desistance process', *American Sociological Review*, 63: 225–38

Lipsey, M.W., Landenberger, N.A. & Wilson, S.J. (2007) *Effects of Cognitive-Behavioural Programmes for Criminal Offenders*. Campbell Systematic Reviews, 6. DOI: 10.4073/csr.2007.6

Maruna, S. (2000) 'Desistance from crime and offender rehabilitation: A tale of two research literatures', *Offender Programs Report*, 4, 1: 1–13

Maruna, S. (2001) *Making Good: How Ex-Convicts Reform and Rebuild their Lives*. Washington, DC: American Psychological Association Books

McGuire, J. (2005) 'The Think First programme'. In: M. McMurran & J. McGuire (eds) *Social Problem Solving and Offending*. Chichester: UK Wiley, pp. 183–206

McNeill, F. (2005) 'Remembering probation in Scotland', *Probation Journal*, 52, 1: 23–38

McNeill, F. (2006) 'A desistance paradigm for offender management', *Criminology and Criminal Justice*, 6, 1: 39–62

McNeill, F. (2011) 'Probation, credibility and Justice', *Probation Journal*, 58, 1: 9–22

McNeill, F. & Weaver, B. (2010) *Changing Lives? Desistance Research and Offender Management*. Glasgow: The Scottish Centre for Crime and Justice Research

Merrington, S. & Stanley, S. (2004) '"What works"? Revisiting the evidence in England and Wales', *Probation Journal*, 51, 1: 7–20

Ministry of Justice (MoJ) (2010) 'Offender Management caseload statistics 2009', *Ministry of Justice Statistics Bulletin*. London: Ministry of Justice

Nellis, M. (2004) 'Into the Field of Corrections": The end of English Probation in the early 21st century?', *Cambrian Law Review*, 35: 115–33

Padfield, N. & Maruna, S. (2006) 'The revolving door at the prison gate: Exploring the dramatic increase in recalls to prison', *Criminology and Criminal Justice*, 6, 3: 329–52

Robinson, G. & McNeill, F. (2004) 'Purposes matter: Examining the "ends of probation"'. In G. Mair (ed.) *What Matters in Probation*. Cullompton: Willan Publishing, pp. 277–304

Smith, D. & Vanstone, M. (2002) 'Probation and social justice', *British Journal of Social Work*, 32, 6: 815–30

Smith, D.J. (2007) 'Crime and the life course'. In: M. Maguire, R. Morgan & R. Reiner (eds) *Oxford Handbook of Criminology*, 4th edn. Oxford: Oxford University Press, pp. 641–87

Vanstone, M. (2004) *Supervising Offenders in the Community: A History of Probation Theory and Practice*. Aldershot: Ashgate

Vaughan, B. (2007) 'The internal narrative of desistance', *British Journal of Criminology*, 47, 3: 390–404

Ward, T. & Maruna, S. (2007) *Rehabilitation: Beyond the Risk-Paradigm*. London: Routledge

6 Prisons and the abolitionist debate

Key issues

- Explain the development of prisons
- Why and how is the prison system in crisis?
- What is the abolitionist debate?

Introduction

How a nation reacts to crime and specifically how it punishes or fails to punish criminals reflect the values of a society. As Nelson Mandela states: 'no one truly knows a nation until one has been inside its jails. A nation should be judged not by how it treats its highest citizens but its lowest ones' (Mandela, 1995: 217).

The aim of this chapter is to highlight the key events that led to the transformation of the prison system, focusing mainly on England and Wales (issues relating to the current prison system in Northern Ireland and Scotland will also be discussed). The following sections will trace the rise of the modern prison as we know it, and conclude by addressing new ways of approaching crime and punishment by discussing prison abolitionism. In the process of mapping the developments of incarceration over the last two centuries the aim of this chapter is to provide an introduction to the central issues that are connected with this topic.

History of prisons

Prior to 1775, prison was used sparingly as a punishment. When it was used, sentences were short and confined to those found guilty of offences such as manslaughter, fraud and those waiting to be sent into exile. During the eighteenth century, prisons existed in three forms: debtors' prisons such as the Dickensian Marshalsea; the county or borough gaol; and houses of correction or bridewells, where the poor were supposed to be put to work. By the 1770s and 1780s the idea had developed that prisons could offer more than just detention.

In 1774, the *Discharge Prisoners Act* allowed for the payment of the fees of prisoners who were acquitted at their trials, and the *Health of Prisoners Act* required prisons to be ventilated, regularly cleaned and that prisoners were provided with baths and medical facilities. By 1776, the principles of reformation were beginning to be reflected in the workings of the convict prison. In 1777, John Howard published the *State of Prisons in England and Wales*, and it was this book that had the widest impact on prison reform. Reflecting growing revulsion against the current prison conditions, the *Penitentiary Act, 1779* was introduced. In 1784, an Act of Parliament called for the need to have separate cells in all new prisons, and two national penitentiaries (male and female) were created.

The rise of the prison

The use of prison as a direct punishment of the court can be linked to the reduction in the use of transportation in the early nineteenth century and its ending in 1868 (Godfrey & Cox, 2008). By the 1850s and 1860s only a small number of convicts were being transported, the rest being imprisoned. To provide for this, the government established the *convict prison system* in which convicts served sentences of penal servitude. Instead of being transported to the colonies, two *Penal Servitude Acts* in 1853 and 1854 endorsed the convict prison system.

Two different types of rehabilitation strategies emerged on to the prison landscape, which became known as the Silent/Auburn and the Separate/Philadelphia system. In the Auburn model, prisoners were put to work in large communal workrooms but were forbidden to talk to each other and were punished harshly if found doing so. The second tradition was based more on the model of Christian monasticism. Prisoners were confined to individual cells, and were not to come into contact with other prisoners, nor talk to staff (Johnson, 2006; Sharpe, 1988).

In 1816, the first government-run prison, the Millbank penitentiary, opened in London. It was constructed to hold 1,000 prisoners awaiting transportation. Prisoners were held in seclusion for the first half of the sentence and then worked in association. In the following years, the regime became more severe, focusing on solitude and isolation. The demise of Millbank led to the creation of a new adult 'model' prison at Pentonville in 1843, with over 500 identical cells in each of which a prisoner was to live in silence. On entering Pentonville, prisoners' names were replaced with numbers, their heads were shaved, they wore identical prison uniforms and were placed in identical cells. Prisoners wore hoods when they emerged from their cells and sat in separate stalls in chapel (McGowen, 1998). The construction of the walls hindered communication between prisoners, and even the guards wore padded shoes so that they would not disturb the prevailing silence. Each cell measured exactly the same, at 13 feet deep, 7 feet wide and 9 feet high. For a regime that was intended to individualise punishment it did its best to erase any trace of individuality. Pentonville became the new model prison of the Victorian era. In the end, Pentonville's demise was relatively swift, and by the mid-1850s it became a convict depot like Millbank. The 1930 Prison Rules finally abolished the practice of separate solitary confinement for the first months of a long sentence.

As this chapter has demonstrated, the mid-nineteenth century saw a number of key transformations in the history and development of prisons in England: from arbitrary state involvement in penal practice to a rationalised and centralised state-organised system; from very little differentiation between criminal groups to the classification and categorisation of prisons and prisoners into separate groups – men and women, adults and young offenders, remand and convicted – requiring specialised forms of intervention. Among these processes the prison emerged as the 'dominant instrument for changing undesirable behaviour and became the favoured form of punishment' (Cohen, 1985: 13).

The next section will examine the role of prisons today and engage in a discussion of the rationale behind the rise of private prisons in England and Wales.

Prisons today

> There is a major 'geological fault' in the prison landscape . . . the 'fault' is the unpredictable and volatile size of the prison population.
>
> (Sir Brian Cubbon, former Permanent Secretary,
> Home Office, quoted in Morgan, 1992: 236)

The prison population in England and Wales dropped from a high of over 30,000 in 1877 – when the *Prison Act* was passed —to a low point of a little over 9,000 at the end of the First World War. During this period from 1908 to 1939 the prison population of England and Wales fell from 22,029 to 11,086 – or, in terms of the numbers of prisoners per 100,000 of the general population, from 63 to 30 (Rutherford, 1988). This period saw the prison population halve, and as a result around twenty prisons had to be closed down despite the fact that the crime rate in this period actually increased by around 100 per cent. Indeed, this is the longest sustained period of decarceration in penal history. In contrast, the story since the Second World War has been one of expansion, and growth in the prison population has been referred to as the 'crisis in prison numbers' (Cavadino & Dignan, 2006: 26). Between 1995 and 2009, the prison population in England and Wales grew by 32,500 or 66 per cent (Prison Reform Trust, 2009).

There are currently 140 prisons in England and Wales. Male prisoners are placed in one of four security categories – A, B, C or D – and are allocated to prisons according to the nature of their offence and the level of security required for their safe containment and control. Women are categorised simply for open or closed conditions apart from women designated as category A.

There are 14 women's prisons (none in Wales, which means that all Welsh women prisoners are outside their home country), and seven are mother and baby units.

The prison system is facing a crisis, including problems of overcrowding. The consequences include a reduction in prison activities and work and educational provision, total lockdowns and the placing of offenders on a prison ship, HMP *Weare*. The prison system has been failing to cope with the rising prison population, and in every one of the years since 1995 the prison system has been overcrowded (NOMS, 2010). Overcrowding means that over 12,000 prisoners are being held two to a cell that was designed for one. Many of these cells have unscreened toilets, which fail to provide even the most basic of human dignity.

Across the jurisdictions there are similarities and differences in the structure and organisation of the criminal justice system, and in turn the running of the prison system. The following section will briefly outline the prison estate in Northern Ireland and Scotland.

Prisons in Northern Ireland

In Northern Ireland the operation of criminal justice has been connected to the impact of 'the Troubles'. The signing of the 1998 Good Friday/Belfast Agreement (GFA) and the early release of most politically motivated prisoners led to a belief that a modern prison service would emerge. However, the shadow of the past still hangs over the operations of the prison system in Northern Ireland, and a recent review of the system called for 'fundamental change and transformation' (Owers *et al.*, 2011).

Northern Ireland now has three prisons: HMP Maghaberry, HMP Magilligan and Hydebank Wood, Young Offender Centre (YOC). Since June 2004, there has been no separate facility for female prisoners in Northern Ireland; women are accommodated in a unit on the grounds of Hydebank Wood, YOC. The prison population is rising, and in 2012 there were 1,739 people in prison in Northern Ireland, compared with 1,482 on the same date in 2010 and 1,301 in 2005 (Owers *et al.*, 2011), and all the prisons are operating beyond capacity.

Prisoners on remand account for over half of the population. One-third of prisoners are serving a life sentence and around one-quarter have sentences of two years or less. The range of security levels at Maghaberry is inappropriate to cater for the range of offenders. In practice this means that 'someone serving five days for fine default receives the same security regime as someone serving a 10-year sentence for serious assault' (CJINI, 2009: v) (see also Wahidin *et al.*, 2012 for a more in-depth analysis of prisons in Northern Ireland).

Specific concerns have been raised regarding the conditions of women prisoners in Northern Ireland (Scraton & Moore, 2005). These concerns have followed from high-profile deaths in custody (see case study at the end of this chapter). It has been noted that the overriding emphasis on security in Northern Ireland means that there have been failures to attend to other aspects of need (Owers *et al.*, 2011; Scraton & Moore, 2005).

The economic cost of imprisonment in Northern Ireland is higher than in other UK jurisdictions. In 2009/10 the average cost per prison place stood at £78,750, significantly higher than in England and Wales, where costs average £40,378 per prisoner per annum, and Scotland, where the average ranges from £31,000 to £40,000.[1] Staff costs account for the largest proportion of operating costs in Northern Ireland (71 per cent), compared to 44 per cent in Scotland (HMCIP Scotland, 2011), and this is linked to historically high staffing ratios (Owers *et al.*, 2011).

Prisons in Scotland

The Scottish Prison Service is an executive agency of the Scottish Government tasked with managing prisons in Scotland. On 23 March 2012, the total prison population stood at 8,679, and women comprised 361 of the total. There are currently 13 publicly managed prisons and two privately managed prisons in Scotland. Cornton Vale is the main female prison, but female offenders are also held in HMP Greenock. There are current plans to create reintegration units for small numbers of female prisoners in Aberdeen and Inverness prisons to allow them to access local community services as they approach release.

As in the cases of Northern Ireland and England and Wales, the prison population is rising and Scotland imprisons more of its population today than it has since records of the imprisonment rate began. The prison population has grown by more than 20 per cent since the start of the twenty-first century, increasing from an average daily population of 5,833 in 2000/1 to 7,183 in 2006/7. The Government estimates that with no changes in current practices, the prison population will grow steadily to 8,700 in less than ten years (2016/17). The figure has already peaked at over 8,000 on a number of occasions (Prison Reform Trust, 2011).

At the time of writing there were 157 prisoners per 100,000 of Scottish population (Prison Reform Trust, 2011). Less than ten years ago that figure was 118. The Scottish imprisonment rate is near the top of European league tables for prison use (see Table 6.1). Table 6.2 lists the countries with the most prisoners.

This section has outlined prisons in different jurisdictions but also illustrates that this society has one of the highest per capita prison populations in Western Europe. The next section will examine the rise of the private prison.

Table 6.1 Rates of imprisonment per 100,000

Scotland	**157**
England & Wales	**155**
Portugal	121
Northern Ireland	**97**
Republic of Ireland	95
Germany	87
Switzerland	70
Finland	59
Iceland	47

Source: Adapted from the International Centre for Prison Studies: http://www.prisonstudies.org/info/worldbrief

Table 6.2 Countries with the most prisoners

Ranking	Countries	Total prison population
1	United States of America	2,266,832
2	China	1,640,000
3	Russian Federation	738,400
4	Brazil	514,582
5	India	368,998
6	Iran	250,000
7	Thailand	234,678
8	Mexico	230,943
9	South Africa	157,375
10	Ukraine	153,508
11	Indonesia	141,689
12	Turkey	132,369
13	Vietnam	113,018
14	Ethiopia	112,361
15	Philippines	104,710
16	United Kingdom: England & Wales	87,028
17	Poland	84,799
18	Colombia	84,444
19	Pakistan	75,586
20	Spain	70,840

Source: © International Centre for Prison Studies 2012
* Statistics are not necessarily from the same year but represent the most recent figures available

Privatisation of prisons

It should be noted from the outset that private prisons are not a new phenomenon. Throughout the nineteenth and into the early twentieth century, contract and lease agreements between prison authorities and private entrepreneurs were common, either for the use of prison labour or for transportation (Borna, 1986; Dilulio, 1990; McConville, 1998; Ryan & Ward, 1989).

The term 'prison privatisation' is normally used to describe the contracting out of prison operations from the state to private providers. It includes prisoner escort services, prison work programmes, electronic monitoring of offenders released from prison, the financing of prison construction and, most controversially of all, the management and operation of prisons (Mehigan & Rowe, 2007).

The development of privatisation

Legislation has played an important part in the legitimating of privatisation. The Home Office Green Paper of 1988 provided a legal basis for experimenting with private sector involvement in the system and escort service. The support for privatisation was further endorsed in *Section 84 of the Criminal Justice Act 1991*, which authorised the contracting out of the new remand prisons. Shortly thereafter, the security company Group 4 Remand Services Ltd received a five-year contract for managing the HMP Wolds remand prison. The prison opened on 5 April 1992 and, two months later, in July, the Act was amended to allow the contracting out of all new prisons, for remand as well as for convicted prisoners (Ryan & Ward, 1989).

England and Wales have taken a leading position in Europe with regard to private sector involvement in the prison system. Since 1988, the concept of privately managed prisons has become increasingly accepted, and the UK has now become what one private prison company has described as 'as one of the largest private correctional market in the world' (http://www.geogroup.com/:1). In 2009, the private sector in England and Wales managed 10.8 per cent of the prisoner population, with over 9,070 prisoners held in private prisons (*NOMS Monthly Bulletin*, 31 July 2009).

Proponents for privatisation claim that it is the best way to decrease costs and construct new and better-designed prisons more quickly (Hutton, 1990; Logan, 1990). Advocates also contend that private prison services can operate more efficiently, because of less bureaucratic 'red tape' and higher motivation to control costs; they also claim that private prisons are better, cheaper more hygienic or more efficiently operated. However, according to a parliamentary written answer (Hansard, House of Commons Written Answers, 9 January 2007: Col. 546W), the costs of private prisons per place are higher than public sector prisons in most categories (see Table 6.3).

Objections to private prisons are wide-ranging. They include fears that the drive for profit can result in cuts in staffing costs, with commensurate reductions in officer–prisoner interaction, time out of cell for prisoners and security for both staff and prisoners. Above all, many people believe that it is morally and ethically unacceptable for private individuals to profit from punishment. Examination of the Universal Declaration of Human Rights shows that privatisation of prisons by way of contracting out management and custody is

Table 6.3 Costs of private prisons

Function	Contracted sector, cost per place, £000s	Public sector, cost per place, £000s
Male Category B	26,813	25,881
Male Category C	20,855	21,976
Female Closed	44,400	34,617
Male Juvenile	48,669	42,143
Male Local	33,805	31,912

Source: Hansard, House of Commons Written Answers, 9 January 2007: Col. 546W

not in accordance with international human rights law. Following a complex argument, starting from Article 21 (the will of the people is the basis of authority of government) and Article 7 (all persons are equal before the law are entitled to equal protection of the law), Palley (1993: 31–2) concludes that 'the responsibility of the State does not permit it to sub-delegate the power of giving effect to restrictions on personal liberty, including having custody of prisoners'.

In most countries prison privatisation has been introduced to cope with rising prison populations and overcrowding problems. Up to now the use of private prisons has become a convenient way to provide an immediate and flexible answer to a persistent penal problem. However, the real issue is not about whether private prisons are managed more effectively and efficiently than private ones, or vice versa. The concept of the prison as a 'marketplace' and a business has changed the nature of prisons as a state-run institution (Feeley, 1991). Moreover, without challenging the legitimacy of the prison system or addressing current criminal justice police about why so many additional prison places are needed, privatisation will at best only bring temporary relief to prison overcrowding. Decarceration and reductionism may be difficult political options in the current punitive climate in which a 'get tough' policy towards criminals has become political. Nevertheless, in relation to the search for reductionist measures, the contracting out of the management of prisons is ultimately a counterproductive strategy. The next section will highlight some of the controversial issues in prison.

The prison population

The total prison population of England and Wales in April 2011 was 84,345. Out of the total 79,630 are men and 4,190 are women. Women represent 6 per cent of the total prison population. Women prisoners are usually held further away from home then men, which can make it difficult for them to maintain contact with their families. Carlen (1983), Sim (1990) and Wahidin (2005) also identified that women in prison are placed under higher levels of surveillance, regulation and control than men. Women are more disciplined than men for infractions that would be tolerated in male prisons. In 2001, women were charged with offences against discipline at a rate of 224 offences per 100 women compared with 160 per 100 men (Butler & Kousoulou, 2006). Women prisoners are five times more likely to have mental health problems than women in the general population (Plugge *et al.*, 2006). The net of the criminal justice system captures those women who have experiences of social exclusion, abuse, mental health difficulties and substance use or dependency. Of all the women who are sent to prison, 37 per cent have attempted suicide at some time in their life, the majority have experienced domestic violence and a third have experienced sexual abuse (Corston, 2007).

Just over a quarter of the male prison population (15 per cent Black, 7 per cent Mixed and 2 per cent Chinese or Other) and 29 per cent of the female prison population (19 per cent Black, 3 per cent Asian, 4 per cent Mixed and 3 per cent Chinese or Other) were from BME groups (MOJ, 2009). One in eight of the people in prison are foreign nationals (MOJ, 2009) and six out of ten foreign national prisoners are serving sentences of more than four years. There was a 152 per cent increase in foreign national prisoners in the ten years to 2004, compared to a 55 per cent increase in British nationals.

Costs of prison

The costs of accommodating individual prisoners and the variations across the United Kingdom have already been discussed. The government expenditure on imprisonment in England and Wales increased from £2.843 billion in 1995 to £4.325 billion in 2007 (Prison Reform Trust, 2009). It is more expensive to build a prison than it is to build a primary school, at £3.4 million. Despite significant expenditure and the underpinning rationale to make prison work, there is very little evidence that prison does actually work, 'at least when measured against its official aims' (Sim, 2009, cited in Scott & Codd, 2010: 4).

Even on its own terms the fact that prison does 'not work' is clearly illustrated by reconviction rates, which show that prison is not the most effective in deterring and rehabilitating those who come in conflict with the law. For example, the Social Exclusion Report (2002) summarised that in the UK 'of those prisoners released in 1997, 58 per cent were convicted of another crime within two years. Thirty-six per cent were back inside on another prison sentence.' Similar figures show that in 2010, 49 per cent of adults are reconvicted within one year of being released, and for those serving sentences of less than 12 months this increased to 61 per cent. Fifty-four per cent of women leaving prison were reconvicted within one year, and for those serving sentences of less than 12 months this increased to 64 per cent. For those women who had served more than ten previous custodial sentences the reoffending rate rose to 90 per cent (MOJ 2010).

Critics of the prison system range across the whole spectrum, from those who would reduce the use of imprisonment or abolish altogether to those who would greatly extend its use and increase the severity of its punitive effect. The previous sections have examined the changing contours of the prison landscape. The final section will discuss the abolitionist perspective to find a new vision for the future of prisons and how we use them.

Abolitionism

> Abolitionism is a stance. It is the attitude of saying 'no'. This does not mean that the 'no' will have an immediate outcome in practice. A 'no' to prisons will not occur in our time. But as a *stance* it is viable and important. When I wrote *The Politics of Abolition* in 1974, and again when I published the last edition of *Prison on Trial* in 2006, I was certainly preoccupied with the strategies of achieving concrete abolition. But I was also preoccupied with fostering and developing an abolitionist stance, a constant and deeply critical attitude to prisons and penal systems.
>
> (Mathiesen, 2008: 33–39)

Abolitionism comes from the verb 'to abolish' or 'to do away'; it can also mean to put an end to the existence or practice to a custom or institution. In criminology and criminal justice, the term 'abolition' ranges from the attempt to *'abolish'*, or *'to bring about radical change'* to punitive responses to crime and punishment (McLaughlin & Muncie, 2006). Abolitionism is not a cohesive theoretical and political movement. It is a philosophy, a way of critically rethinking crime, punishment and the criminal justice system (Bianchi & Van Swaningen, 1986; Hulsman, 1991). Early abolitionists advocated an alternative vision for criminal justice politics, and neo-abolitionists, although accepting many of the abolitionist principles, reject both the concept of crime and penalty and instead look at social harms.

Towards abolitionism

In the move to reconfigure the debate of crime and punishment the prison abolitionist movement focuses on some of these areas. Firstly, abolitionists would argue for a moratorium on the prison-building programme and in turn redefine the terms and direction of the debate about the prisons/industrial/state complex (Mathiesen, 2000; Ruggiero, 2010). Secondly, abolitionists challenge the role of the prison within contemporary political and popular consciousness. Thirdly, abolitionists critically examine the culture of the total institution and aim to redefine the terms, meanings and direction of the prison debate in order to find an alternative, which is grounded in human rights and social justice for all. There are those too who would argue for selective abolitionism (Hudson,

1993), on the basis of individual vulnerability or because certain offences do not cause serious harm.

However, abolitionists have consistently been accused and dismissed as being, naive, idealistic, and for having a 'preoccup[ation] with abolishing or minimising state intervention rather than attempting to make it more effective, responsive and accountable' (Matthews, 1990, cited in Sim, 1994: 265). Abolitionists have rejected the above criticism and have clearly demonstrated that the abolitionist philosophy has influenced political debates and effected change through social policies in terms of making the state more accountable. Indeed, the concept of 'selective abolitionism' has been applied in an official report on women's imprisonment (Corston, 2007). This report concluded by stating: 'the existing system of women's prisons should be dismantled and replaced by smaller secure units for the minority of women from whom the public requires protection' (Corston, 2007: 5).

Conclusion

This chapter has explored the changing function and role that has given ascendancy to the prison of the present outlining some of the salient developments in the penal industrial complex. Its history has been the focus of controversy and debate.

Prisons undoubtedly generate significant levels of social harm and collateral damage. The very processes of classifying and labelling the person as a criminal and creating prisons as places for and as punishment leads to wider social harms – such as the loss of employment, reduced job prospects etc. These harms tend to 'fall disproportionately on relatively vulnerable members of society' (Hillyard *et al.*, 2004). Prisons are places that are counterproductive to the reform and rehabilitation of the person. From 1990 to 2012 there were 2,930 deaths in prison in England and Wales. In 2002, there were more African Caribbean entrants to prison (over 11,500) than there were entering UK universities (around 8,000) (HMCIP, 2009).

As the UK prison population spirals towards a projected figure of over 110,000 there is a call that it should be replaced with other means of responding to troubles, conflicts and social harms. By questioning the proliferation and the centrality of the use of imprisonment in society, and by questioning the idea of prisons as being reformative or able to reduce harm or control crime, we can begin to create a new vision and a new language around crime, punishment and imprisonment. This new vision should be grounded in a human rights and a social justice agenda (Fitzgerald & Sim, 1979). In the words of the Dutch abolitionist Willem de Hann, the problem is that 'the prison is counter-productive, difficult to control and [is] itself a major social problem' (De Hann, 1990: 53).

Glossary

Abolitionism – a theoretical and political perspective that argues that the penal system creates social problems and social harms. Abolitionism calls for a new approach to the current ways of responding to and thinking about crime.

Decarceration – refers to policies that aim to reduce the numbers of offenders in prison by providing alternative measures to incarceration.

Incapacitation – is a theory of punishment that proposes that by removing the offending from society there will be a simultaneous reduction in crime.

Penitentiary – is a term used to describe the first convict prison in the early nineteenth century. The term draws upon the Christian term 'penitence'.

Case study

In the care of the State?

On 7 September 2002, 19-year-old Annie Kelly died by hanging in a Northern Irish prison. She had been in conflict with the law since the age of 13, committed to prison on 28 occasions, diagnosed with a personality disorder and had a history of self-harm. She refused food and water, lacerated her arms, banged her head, inserted metal objects under her skin and strangled herself with ligatures until she lost consciousness.

Annie Kelly was placed in the punishment block for assaulting officers. The record of incidents involving Annie Kelly between 10 July 1997 and 29 July 2002 shows 30 assaults on staff, 4 on other prisoners, 40 incidents of self-harm, 52 wrecked cells, 17 threats and 42 'miscellaneous', non-specified incidents. Her cell consisted of an open toilet, sink, and bed. A report noted that she had pulled the ceramic hand basin from the wall, removed the taps, and used them as instruments to break through the cell wall. She was returned to the basic punishment regime in a 'dry cell', which meant there was no mattress, no bed, and no pillow. She slept on a raised concrete plinth. On 7 September, Annie Kelly was found hanging by ligatures torn from an anti-suicide blanket from the diamond steel mesh of a window that should have been fully covered by Perspex to make it ligature-free. Further factors contributing to Annie's death were: her isolation for long periods; lack of appropriate female facilities; and the lack of a therapeutic alternative outside prison to meet her complex mental health needs.

The inquest into her death was held before a jury between 10 and 23 November 2004. At the inquest the jury's verdict did not consider that

Annie Kelly died 'by her own act' but that 'defects in the prison system contributed to the death'.

Reasonable precautions that might have avoided Annie's death were:

1.   Window – an anti-ligature window should have been installed.
2.   Observation – given her recent behaviour, clearer guidelines on observation and monitoring may not have afforded Annie the opportunity of making ligatures.
3.   If Annie had been searched at some stage of the day ligatures would have been discovered.
4.   Cell inspection should have been carried out more frequently and thoroughly, especially regarding the window.

Annie Kelly was in the 'care of the State': do you think her death was preventable if reasonable precautions had been taken?

Seminar questions

1.   Explain the rise in the prison population.
2.   Is the prison failing to deter and rehabilitate those who come into conflict with the law?
3.   List a number of reasons for the crisis facing the prison system.

Further reading

Scott, D. & Codd, H. (2010) *Controversial Issues in Prisons*. Milton Keynes: Open University Press

This textbook explores eight of the most controversial aspects of imprisonment in England and Wales. It looks at the people who are sent to prison and what happens to them when they are incarcerated. Each chapter examines a different dimension of the prison population and makes connections between the personal troubles and vulnerabilities of those confined.

Sim, J. (2009) *Punishment and Prisons: Power and the Carceral State*. London: Sage

An excellent book that critiques the development of penal policy from 1974 to the present day by placing the argument within a discussion of penal policy and state power.

Ruggiero, V. (2010) *Penal Abolitionism*. Oxford: Oxford University Press

This book examines the origin of abolitionism and its philosophy, and reviews the literature on penal abolitionism from the 1960s to the 1980s. It examines in particular how abolitionist perspectives developed, their philosophical foundations and the social and political context of abolitionist ideas and perspectives.

Further information can be obtained from the following websites

ICOPA – International Conference on Penal Abolition: http://www. actionicopa.org/
A useful website that gives information about the organisation Penal Abolition.

INQUEST http://www.inquest.org.uk/INQUEST
This is a charity that provides a free advice service to bereaved people on contentious deaths and their investigation, with a particular focus on deaths in custody.

No More Prisons http://www.nomoreprisons.com.au/index.html
A grassroots organisation that provides details of reports and debates on the pains of imprisonment.

Women in Prison http://www.womeninprison.org.uk/
The website is comprehensive, with relevant links to articles, thematic reports and statistics on the female prison population. Women in Prison supports and campaigns for women offenders and ex-offenders.

Bibliography

Bianchi, H. & van Swaningen, R. (eds) (1986) *Abolitionism*. Amsterdam: Free University Press

Borna, S. (1986) 'Free enterprise goes to prison', *British Journal of Criminology*, 26, 4: 321–34

Butler, P. & Kousoulou, D. (2006) *Women at Risk: The Mental Health of Women in Contact with the Judicial System*. London: London Development Centre

Carlen, P. (1983) *Women's Imprisonment: A Study of Social Control*. London: Routledge, Kegan Paul

Cavadino, M. and Dignan, J. (2006) *Penal Systems: A Comparative Approach*. London: Sage

Cohen, S. (1985) *Visions of Social Control*. London: Polity Press

Corston, J. (2007) *A Review of Women with Particular Vulnerabilities in the Criminal Justice System*. London: Home Office

Criminal Justice Inspection Northern Ireland (CJINI) (2009) *Report on an Unannounced Full Follow-up Inspection of Maghaberry Prison 19–23 January 2009*. Belfast: CJINI

De Haan, W. (1990) *The Politics of Redress: Crime, Punishment and Penal Abolition*. London: Unwin Hyman

Dilulio, J. Jr (1990) 'The duty to govern: A critical perspective on the private management of prisons and jails'. In: C. Douglas & C. McDonald (eds) *Private Prisons and the Public Interest*. New Brunswick, NJ: Rutgers University Press, pp. 155–78

Feeley, M. (1991) 'The privatization of punishment in historical perspective'. In W. Gormley (ed.) *Privatization and its Alternatives*. Madison, WI: University of Wisconsin Press, pp. 199–225

Fitzgerald, M. & Sim, J. (1979) *British Prisons*. Oxford: Blackwell

Geo Group Inc. (2012) www.geogroup.com [accessed 10 June 2012]

Godfrey, B. & Cox, D. (2008) 'The "Last Fleet": Crime, reformation and punishment in Western Australia', *Australian and New Zealand Journal of Criminology*, 41, 2: 236–58

Her Majesty's Chief Inspector of Prisons (2009) *Race Relations in Prisons*. London: HM Inspectorate of Prisons

Her Majesty's Chief Inspector of Prisons for Scotland (2011) *Annual Report 2010–2011*. Glasgow

Hillyard, P., Sim, J., Tombs, S. & Whyte, D. (2004) 'Leaving a "Stain upon a Silence": Contemporary criminology and the politics of dissent', *British Journal of Criminology*, 44: 369–90

Hudson, B.A. (1993) *Penal Policy and Social Justice*. London: Macmillan

Hulsman, L. (1991) 'The abolitionist case: Alternative crime policies', *Israel Law Review*, 10, 1: 681–709

Hutton, T. (1990) 'Privatisation of prisons'. In W.J. Murphy & E. Dison (eds) *Are Prisons any Better? Twenty Years of Reform*. Newbury Park, CA: Sage, pp. 111–27

Johnson, H. (2006) '"Buried Alive": Representations of the Separate System in Victorian England'. In P. Mason (ed.) *Captured by the Media: Prison Discourse in Popular Culture*. Cullompton: Willan Publishing, pp. 103–22

Logan, C.H. (1990) *Private Prisons: Pros and Cons*. New York: Oxford University Press

Mandela, N. (1995) *A Long Walk to Freedom: The Autobiography of Nelson Mandela*. London: Little Brown

Mathiesen, T. (2000) 'Towards the 21st century: Abolition – an impossible dream?' In W. Gordon West & R. Morris (eds) *The Case for Penal Abolition*. Toronto: Canadian Scholars' Press Inc., pp. 333–57

Mathiesen, T. (2008), 'The Abolitionist Stance', plenary paper at the XII International Conference on Penal Abolition, King's College, London, 23 July.

McConville, S. (1998) 'The Victorian prison, 1865–1965'. In N. Morris and D.J. Rothman (eds) *The Oxford History of the Prison – The Practice of Punishment in Western Society*. New York: Oxford University Press, pp. 117–51

McGowen, R. (1998) 'The well-ordered prison, England, 1780–1865'. In N. Morris and D.J. Rothman (eds) *The Oxford History of the Prison – The Practice of Punishment in Western Society*. New York: Oxford University Press, pp. 71–100

McLaughlin, E. & Muncie, J. (2006) *The Sage Dictionary of Criminology*. London: Sage

Mehigan, J. and Rowe, A. (2007) 'Problematizing prison privatization: An overview of the debate'. In: Y. Jewkes (ed.) *Handbook on Prisons*. Cullompton: Willan Publishing, pp. 356–76

Ministry of Justice (2009) *Statistics on Race and the Criminal Justice System 2007/2008: A Ministry of Justice Publication under Section 95 of the Criminal Justice Act 1991*. London: Ministry of Justice

Ministry of Justice (2010) *Compendium of Reoffending Statistics and Analysis*. London: Ministry of Justice

Morgan, R. (1992) 'Following Woolf: The prospects for prisons policy', *Journal of Law and Society*, 19, 2: 231–50

National Offender Management System (NOMS) (2009) *Safer Custody News, July/August*. London: NOMS

National Offender Management System (NOMS) (2010) *Prison Population and Accommodation Briefing, 18th June 2010*. London: NOMS

Owers, A., Leighton, P., McGrory, C., McNeill, F. & Wheatley, P. (2011) *Review of the Northern Ireland Prison Service*. Belfast: Prison Review Team

Palley, C. (1993) 'The administration of justice and the human rights of detainees: 'The possible utility, scope and structure of a special study on the issue of privatization of prisons', UN Commission on Human Rights, online, UN doc. E/CN.4/Sub.2/1993/21

Plugge, E., Douglas, N. & Fitzpatrick, R. (2006) *The Health of Women in Prison*. Oxford: Department of Public Health, University of Oxford

Prison Reform Trust (2009) *Bromley Briefing Paper*. London: PRT

Prison Reform Trust (2011) *Bromley Briefing Paper*. London: PRT

Rutherford, A. (1988) *Prisons and the Process of Justice*. Oxford: Oxford Paperbacks

Ruggiero, V. (2010) *Penal Abolitionism*. Oxford: Oxford University Press

Ryan, M. & Ward, T. (1989) *Privatisation and the Penal System*. Milton Keynes: Open University Press

Scott, D. & Codd, H. (2010) *Controversial Issues in Prisons*. Milton Keynes: Open University Press

Scraton, P. & Moore, L. (2005) *The Hurt Inside: The Imprisonment of Women and Girls in Northern Ireland*. Belfast: NIHRC

Sharpe, J.A. (1988) 'A history of crime in England c.1300–1924'. In P. Rock (ed.) *A History of British Criminology, British Journal of Criminology* 28, 2: 124–37

Sim, J. (1990) *Medical Power in Prisons*. Buckingham: Open University Press

Sim, J. (1994) 'The abolitionist approach: A British perspective'. In A. Duff, S. Marshall, R.E. Dobash and R.P. Dobash (eds) *Penal Theory and Practice: Tradition and Innovation in Criminal Justice*. Manchester: Manchester University Press, pp. 263–91

Sim, J. (2009) *Punishment and Prisons: Power and the Carceral State*. London: Sage

Social Exclusion Unit (2002) *Reducing Re-offending by Ex-prisoners*. London: Cabinet Office

Wahidin, A. (2005) *Older Women and the Criminal Justice System: Running Out of Time*. London: Jessica Kingsley Press

Wahidin, A., Moore, L., & Convery, U. (2012) Unlocking a Locked-Down Regime: The Role of Penal Policy and Administration in Northern Ireland and the Challenges of Change, in A. Wahidin (ed.), Special Issue *On the Legacy of Conflict and the Impact on the Northern Irish Criminal Justice System* in *The Howard Journal of Criminal Justice*, 51, 5. December 2012.

7 Youth justice

Contexts, systems and practices

Key issues

- Why is there a separate justice system for young people?
- Should youth justice systems focus more on issues of welfare?
- Why has there been a rise in the number of young people in custody in parts of the UK?

Introduction

This chapter explores the *youth justice system* as a distinct but constituent part of the criminal justice system. Separate 'youth justice systems' aim to recognise that, while children and young people may be legally responsible for a crime as reflected in the age of criminal responsibility, the type of intervention required differs from adults who have transgressed the law. Typically, therefore, youth justice systems tend to combine aspects of a welfare-oriented approach with a justice or court-mandated response.

Part of the rationale for a different approach is the recognition that children and young people who become involved in crime also have welfare needs, and they may present with child protection concerns. Secondly, longitudinal data from a range of sources on patterns of offending suggests that most people 'grow out' of crime and that one of the most effective means of preventing further offending is to divert young people from formal processing in the criminal justice system (McAra & McVie, 2007; Muncie, 2009). Therefore many systems place an emphasis on strategies of prevention, diversion and early intervention.

Welfare and/or justice?

Traditionally, approaches towards young offenders have been characterised as either 'welfare' or 'justice' oriented. In reality they are more often a mix of both. Welfare approaches are understood as those focused on meeting the young person's needs, and include an understanding that criminal behaviour is often linked to wider issues of need, such as child poverty or poor educational attainment. Justice oriented approaches, on the other hand, are understood as having a focus on principles such as responsibilisation and retribution, that is, a person (whether young or old) should be held responsible for their actions and 'pay back' to society in the form of a legal sanction, the most severe of which is typically imprisonment.

Very often the line between 'welfare' and 'justice' based approaches is not clear-cut, and indeed Muncie (2006) argues that the rationales for youth justice interventions are often changing and contradictory. Therefore, whether issues relating to youth offending are a matter of welfare, child protection or justice is by no means straightforward. Sometimes the decision on whether a young person is to be treated within the welfare/child protection system or the criminal justice system can depend on the severity of the crime. Also within the various jurisdictions in the United Kingdom there are different approaches to young people and crime and different youth justice systems. Most notably, in Scotland there has traditionally been a stronger 'welfarist' approach to youth justice evident in the 'Children's Hearing System' (discussed later in this chapter).

Age of criminal responsibility

One of the key indicators of the perspective adopted in relation to young people and crime is the age at which children are deemed to be criminally responsible. In England, Wales and Northern Ireland the age of criminal responsibility is ten years of age. In Scotland the age of criminal responsibility is eight years, but under legislation passed in 2010, a child under the age of 12 years cannot be prosecuted for an offence.[1] The relatively low age of criminal responsibility in the United Kingdom can be contrasted with other European countries. In France the age of criminal responsibility is 13 years, in Austria and Slovenia it is 14 years, in Sweden it is 15 years, in Poland 17 years and in Belgium 18 years (Muncie & Goldson, 2006). Looking at these variations, it is clear that the age at which children are deemed to be criminally responsible is not an immutable fact, rather it is a product of social, historical and legal constructions.

One of the key factors influencing the notion of 'criminal responsibility' is the question of whether the person committing the act had the capacity to understand between 'right' and 'wrong'. The age at which children are deemed to have this moral capacity is based on a number of influences, including the teaching of various religions. There have been various critiques of what is considered to be a relatively low age of criminal responsibility within England, Wales, Northern Ireland and Scotland, including the argument that children at this age do not always have the capacity to fully understand the nature and consequences of their actions, in particular any longer-term consequences such as harm and loss of liberty.

Secondly, it is argued that children of this age who commit acts that may be classified as criminal usually have a range of welfare needs that in many cases have been unmet. It is argued that the youth justice system, albeit tailored for youths rather than adults, is not an adequate place through which these needs should be met (Goldson, 2000b; Muncie, 2006).

Calls have been made from time to time to raise the age of criminal responsibility. For example, *Barnardos,* the national children's charity, recently ran the *'Kids Inside'* campaign, which argued that the age of criminal responsibility in England and Wales should be raised from 10 to 12 years (Barnardos, 2010). Despite the fact that England, Wales and Northern Ireland have one of the lowest ages of criminal responsibility for developed countries, there has been reluctance on a public policy level to commit to raising this age. In part this is attributed to what is termed 'punitive populism', a term coined by Bottoms (1995) to describe the manner in which politicians tap into the perceived public appetite for punitive criminal justice approaches.

This was particularly evident in the political debate in the United Kingdom in the 1990s where the Conservative and Labour parties vied for the accolade of the party that was 'tough on crime' (Muncie, 1999). Punitive attitudes towards young offenders in particular were influenced by one of the most notorious cases involving children in the UK, the killing of the toddler James Bulger by two ten-year-olds in 1993.

The Bulger murder

In 1993, in Liverpool a young toddler named James Bulger was abducted from a shopping precinct, having wandered from his mother. The police were quickly alerted, and a major hunt was launched to find the two abductors, who were seen walking from the shopping centre hand in hand with James. The grainy CCTV image was broadcast on national media. Later the next day, James Bulger's body was found beside railway tracks several kilometres from the shopping centre from which he had been abducted. Attention towards the crime was greatly amplified when it emerged that James's two abductors were in fact two ten-year-old boys who had been truanting from school.

Both boys were convicted of the abduction and murder of James Bulger in Preston Crown Court in 1993, and were sentenced to detention 'at Her Majesty's Pleasure'. In the wake of extensive publicity in relation to the case and the decision of the trial judge to allow both Jon Venables' and Robert Thompson's names and photographs to be published, the Home Secretary set a minimum tariff of 15 years for the boys' detention. This was subsequently appealed to the European Court of Human Rights, who ruled that the conduct of the trial and the setting of the tariff by the Home Secretary was in contravention of the European Court of Human Rights (Haydon & Scraton, 2000). In 2001 both Venables and Thompson were released under new identities, and the press is precluded from identifying them. However, evidence of the continued notoriety that the case attracts is seen in the recent controversy surrounding Jon Venables' return to prison on charges of possession of indecent images of children.

Punitive populism and young offenders

The reaction to this crime, including the enduring publicity it attracted, has also had a very real affect both on the manner in which young people and crime are perceived, and indeed the manner in which youth justice policy has been subsequently formulated. Several authors who have written about the youth justice system in England and Wales in the 1990s and 2000s have noted what have been described as trends towards 'adulteration' and increased punitiveness (Goldson, 2000b; Haydon & Scraton, 2002; Muncie, 2008; Scraton, 1997). Manifestations of these trends include the introduction of *Anti-Social Behaviour Orders (ASBOs)* into legislation in England, Scotland and Wales under the *Crime and Disorder Act, 1998* and in Northern Ireland under the *Anti-Social Behaviour (Northern Ireland) Order, 2004*. These civil orders allow for courts to impose restrictions on people involved in anti-social behaviour. 'Anti-social behaviour', a somewhat nebulous term, is defined in legislation as:

> acting in an anti-social manner, that is to say, in a manner that caused or was likely to cause harassment, alarm or distress to one or more persons not of the same household as himself.
>
> (Section 1(a), *Crime and Disorder Act, 1998*)

As these are 'civil orders', the standard of proof required to obtain an order is lower than in a criminal court (where the standard is that of 'beyond reasonable doubt') (Ashworth *et al.*, 1998). In the original legislation various bodies, including police and local authorities, could apply to the court for an ASBO in respect of an individual. Types of restrictions that can be placed on a person on an ASBO include a prohibition on entering certain areas, a requirement to observe a curfew or a prohibition on association with certain individuals. Breaching the terms of an ASBO constitutes a criminal offence. Research has demonstrated an overall breach rate of approximately 40 per cent (Squires & Stephen, 2005).

There has been wide criticism of the use of ASBOs, including the types of behaviour that have been targeted. Young people are the disproportionate recipients of these orders, accounting for approximately three-quarters of all orders issued (Campbell, 2002; Tisdall, 2006). Furthermore, the overly punitive approach to the enforcement of ASBOs in the absence of supports for children and families has been highlighted (Squires & Stephen, 2005). The publication of the pictures of young people subject to ASBOs in the local and national press, breaking with the convention of *in camera* rules in criminal proceedings, where defendants under the age of 18 are usually not identified, has also been the subject of strong critique (Thomas *et al.*, 2004).

As noted, ASBOs are not criminal orders. In many cases the type of behaviour targeted would not meet the threshold for a criminal prosecution. However, once a young person is made subject to an ASBO the breach of this order constitutes a criminal offence. For example, a young person made subject to an ASBO may be prohibited from entering specific areas or associating with certain other young people, but if they are then found to have contravened these prohibitions they can be prosecuted for a criminal offence. Several commentators have therefore argued that ASBOs provide a short-circuited route through which young people are criminalised, and have linked such measures with wider 'institutionalised intolerance' of young people (Muncie, 1999).

Children and young people in custody

Youth custody provision is a distinct part of the youth justice system. In England and Wales there is a mixed range of provision including Secure Training Centres (STCS), Local Authority Secure Children's Homes (LASCHs) and Young Offender Institutions (YOIs). The *Youth Justice Board* is responsible for coordinating the provision of these services, including commissioning and funding of places and a central coordinating placement function for all young people sentenced to custody.[2] The three different types of institutions are intended to cater for different populations of young people, as illustrated in Table 7.1.

The number of children and young people in custody in England and Wales has risen markedly, with an increase of 795 per cent from 1989 to 2009 (Standing Committee for Youth Justice, 2010). A number of reasons have been put forward for this rise, including an extension in the 1990s of the range and length of custodial provisions for under-18s. Increased punitiveness has been linked to political debate regarding which of the then main political parties in England and Wales (Conservative and Labour) were 'tougher on crime'. This was fuelled in part by the public and media reaction to the murder of James Bulger and to wider concerns regarding the perception of crime (Haydon & Scraton, 2000).

Current custodial population in England and Wales

The latest available data on the youth custody population in England and Wales published by the Ministry of Justice indicates a downward trend in the numbers of young people in custody (Ministry of Justice, 2011) (see Figure 7.1).

Table 7.1 Youth custody facilities in England and Wales

Institution type	Population	Description
Secure Training Centre	12–15-year-old males 12–16-year-old females (and sometimes older young people assessed as being especially 'vulnerable')	There are 4 STCs in England and Wales, which are operated by private companies. They have a total capacity for 286 young people
Local Authority Secure Children's Homes	These units generally accommodate young people under the age of 15. They also sometimes accommodate older young people who are deemed to be 'vulnerable'	There are 15 LASCHs in England and Wales. Local authorities operate the majority of these. One secure children home is operated by a private company
Young Offender Institute	Males 15–17-years-old Females 17-years-old	These institutions are run by the Prison Service

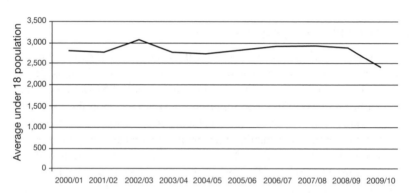

Figure 7.1 Annual custody population (under 18), 2000–2001 to 2009–2010

Source: Ministry of Justice, *Youth Justice Statistics (England and Wales)* (2011): 27

The annual data also provides a breakdown in the type of offences for which young people receive custodial sentences, with offences of violence against the person and robbery constituting the reason for almost half of all custody sentences. Of note also is that 13 per cent of all custodial sentences are given for breaches of statutory orders including Anti-Social Behaviour Orders (ASBOs) (see Figure 7.2).

Research on young people who are sentenced to custody demonstrates high levels of need. Morgan (2010) notes the high incidence of identifiable mental health problems, substance misuse and learning difficulties among the population of young people in custody. In recent years practices within the custodial estate, particularly in England and Wales, have been the subject of concern. There have

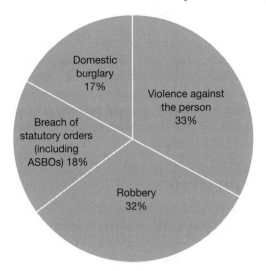

Figure 7.2 Breakdown of offences for which young people (under 18) received a custodial sentence, 2009–2010

Source: Ministry of Justice, *Youth Justice Statistics (England and Wales)* (2011)

been 31 deaths of young people in custody from 1997 to 2011 (Coles, 2011). The majority of deaths are as a result of suicide. However, Gareth Myatt, a 15-year-old boy, died in Rainsbrook Secure Training Centre in 2004 of asphyxiation in the course of a physical restraint (Carlile, 2006). The subsequent report of inquiry into the use of physical restraint, solitary confinement and strip-searching in youth custodial facilities identified a number of areas of concern, including the routine inappropriate use of physical restraint. The report recommended a ban on the use of handcuffs for young offenders and reducing the number of physical restraints by at least half (Carlile, 2006).

The vulnerability of young people in custody is also underlined by documented failures to safeguard young people in these settings. One high profile example of this was the killing of Zahid Mubarek in a racially motivated attack by his cellmate in Feltham Young Offender Institute in 2000. The Home Secretary ordered an inquiry into the circumstances that led to Zahid's death (Keith, 2006). One of the key questions addressed by the inquiry was why Zahid was placed in a cell with another young person with known racist and violent tendencies. (See case study at the end of this chapter for further discussion.)

Prompted by this killing, the *Commission for Racial Equality (CRE)* conducted a formal investigation of the prison service (CRE, 2003), and concluded that the prison service was guilty of racial discrimination. Among its findings the CRE identified that ethnic minority staff experienced discrimination and victimisation, and that there was a systemic failure to tackle these issues within the Prison Service.

Youth justice continuum

If we view the youth justice system as a continuum of interventions, custody and secure provision is at the most intensive or 'sharp' end of this continuum. A whole range of interventions aimed at preventing and reducing offending are targeted towards young people at various other points along this continuum. Again, the precise configuration of services varies in different parts of the United Kingdom, but a number of broad principles guide practice, including an initial focus on *diversion, prevention* and *early intervention.*

Diversion from the criminal justice system

In recognition of the fact that contact with the criminal justice system does not necessarily lead to positive outcomes for young people, there have been broad policy and practice initiatives to *divert* young people away from formal involvement in the criminal justice system. For example, in most jurisdictions provisions exist to allow the police to issue a warning or a reprimand to a young person for criminal behaviour rather than proceeding any further with the case. This effectively means that in such instances the young person's contact with the criminal justice system should end at this point, unless they come to attention for any further matters.

The long-established principle of *diversion* is influenced by understandings gained from the sociological study of deviance and contributions such as *labelling theories.* These theories outline that involvement in the criminal justice system can lead to negative *labelling* effects whereby the young person comes to be viewed by both himself and others as 'criminal' and acts accordingly. This view is supported in one of the most comprehensive studies undertaken on young people and offending, *The Edinburgh Study of Youth Transitions and Crime* (McAra & McVie, 2007; Smith, 2006; Smith & McVie, 2003).

The *Edinburgh Study* is a longitudinal study of a single cohort of young people who started secondary school in Edinburgh in autumn 1998. Its main aim is to investigate the factors that impact on young people's involvement in offending behaviour and in their desistance from offending. Through repeat cohorts of data collection the study explores how a range of factors such as individual development, the social and physical structures of neighbourhoods and interactions with official agencies of social control and law enforcement impact on youth offending. One of the key messages from the study to date is that offending among young people (even offending of a serious and persistent nature) is more likely to be successfully addressed by using strategies of *'minimal intervention and maximum diversion'* (McAra & McVie, 2007: 318). This finding is supported by other international longitudinal research (Huizinga *et al.*, 2003; Tracy & Kempf-Leonard, 1996).

Prevention and early intervention

Alongside diversion a range of youth justice policies and practices are targeted towards *prevention* and *early intervention*. The prevention of crime is one of the main articulated purposes of the youth justice system. Strategies of crime prevention have proliferated in the past two decades, and include practical or *situational* measures such as 'designing out' crime. One example of this is the anti-theft devices that have been developed for cars, which make them much harder to steal. Other crime prevention measures target particular young people who are thought to be *at risk* of offending. Examples of this in England and Wales include the development of *Youth Inclusion Support Panels (YISPs)* and *Youth Inclusion Programmes (YIPs)*, both of which are led and coordinated by local *Youth Offending Teams (YOTS)* (see Box 7.1).

Box 7.1 Prevention – Youth Inclusion Programmes

Youth Inclusion Programmes (YIPs) were established in 2000 in the 'most deprived' areas of England and Wales. The purpose of the programmes was the reintegration of young people deemed to be 'most of risk of offending, truancy or school exclusion' (YJB, 2004: 14). The voluntary programmes aimed to target the 'core 50' young people in local areas deemed to be 'at risk' through a process known as 'ID 50'. YIPs coordinated by local Youth Offending Teams (YOTS) received referrals from a range of local agencies such as police, schools and social services (Mackie *et al.*, 2008). The targets set by the Youth Justice Board for these programmes included a reduction in the arrest rate of the 'core 50' young people by 60 per cent and to reduce recorded crime in the neigbourhood by 50 per cent. The type of preventative work undertaken with young people includes the provision of educational and employment support, engagement in recreational activities and specific targeted work such as addressing anger management. Some critics of the *preventative paradigm* argue that such services should not be coordinated and channelled through agencies within the youth justice system, but should rather should focus on universal and holistic service provision for all young people based on need (Newburn, 2002; Paylor, 2011).

The benefits of effective intervention include the provision of services for young people at an appropriate time and intervening to prevent future problematic behaviours (Whyte, 2009). However, appropriate intervention presents its own challenges, some of which are set out succinctly by Whyte (2009: 100):

Non-intervention should operate on the empirically justifiable premise that family resolution is more likely to be lasting and that many young people 'grow out' of crime with minimal assistance following detection. However, some simply will not and doing 'nothing' may prove to be a missed opportunity to provide constructive and positive help at an early stage, particularly for those with complex needs.

Further challenges include concerns regarding potential net-widening, that is, extending the reach of the criminal justice system and the associated risk of labelling of young people as 'troublesome'.

Risk factors and offending

The decision on which young people should be targeted for interventions and the type of interventions that they receive is determined by their presenting behaviour *and* an assessment of the risk of future involvement in offending. Much of what is termed *risk factor research* or the *risk factor prevention paradigm* is underpinned by the findings of the longitudinal *Cambridge Study of Delinquent Development* (West & Farrington, 1973) and further work carried out by its authors (e.g. Farrington, 1989; 1995; 2000; 2007). Similar longitudinal studies have since been undertaken in other areas, including Australia (Homel, 2005), New Zealand (Fergusson *et al.*, 1993), North America (Wikstrom & Loeber, 1998), Scandinavia (Wikstrom, 1998) and Scotland, as already mentioned (Smith & McAra, 2004), and have led to the identification of a range of risk factors across four key domains, namely: family, school, community and individual.

Family characteristics such as a history of family involvement in criminal behaviour, parental attitudes that condone anti-social and criminal behaviour and poor parental supervision and discipline have been identified as risk factors for future involvement in offending (Farrington, 2007; YJB, 2005). Further contextual factors such as experience of family conflict, low income and poor housing have also been noted. Negative experiences of schooling, such as low achievement (beginning in primary school) and school disorganisation, truanting from school and aggressive behaviour in school have also been linked with involvement in offending (Farrington, 2007; YJB, 2005). Further, an extensive range of literature has pointed to the intersection of social and material disadvantage and involvement in offending and processing through the criminal justice system. Factors such as living in a disadvantaged, high-crime area have been shown to increase the likelihood of future involvement in the criminal justice system. Finally, individual characteristics such as low intelligence, hyperactivity, impulsivity, attitudes and peer friendships have been held to be risk factors that are predictive of future offending (Farrington, 2007).

Critiques of the risk factor prevention paradigm

Critiques of the *risk factor prevention paradigm* point to a number of difficulties with the underpinning evidence base (Haines & Case, 2008; Webster *et al.*, 2006). One of the key areas of criticism relates to interpretation of causality, that is, while a range of *factors* may be present in young people who become involved in offending, making the links between these factors and subsequent criminal involvement is problematic (Haines & Case, 2008). Or, as O'Mahony (2009: 101) notes:

> Most identified risk factors are, in fact, merely correlates of relatively vague proxies for criminality, such as self-reported offending, arrest, conviction or a history of persistent offending.

This leads to questions regarding the *predictive validity* of risk factors, as it is difficult prospectively to predict which people with these characteristics or experiences will become involved in offending (Haines & Case, 2008; McAra & McVie, 2007; Muncie, 2009; Webster *et al.*, 2006). Available evidence also suggests that clusters of risk factors and their interrelationships are likely to be more important than individual factors, and that several factors are likely to overlap – for example, poor school attendance may be linked to poor parental supervision, which may in turn be associated with low educational attainment. Also much of the *risk factor* research has traditionally focused on young white males, and therefore the knowledge base for offenders with a different profile – for example, female, older, black or ethnic minority – is limited (Farrington, 2007; Haines & Case, 2008; Ward & Maruna, 2007).

Perhaps most importantly, it is argued that *risk factors* tend to locate the cause and therefore the solution of the 'problem' at the level of the individual, with an associated tendency of ignoring wider structural factors. So, for example, poor school attainment is viewed as a risk factor but a wider perspective would require an analysis of the opportunities for access to education and inequalities associated therein.

Given that the philosophy and interventions within the criminal justice system are overwhelmingly targeted at the level of the individual (as we have discussed in Chapter 5), it is perhaps unsurprising that individual *responsiblisation* is a core orienting principle. The assessment and management of risk with the core underpinning of risk factor research has become a central organising principle and feature of practice within youth justice systems.

Assessment of risk factors

Practitioners working with young people in the youth justice system in England and Wales use the ASSET assessment tool to assess the risks to and needs of young people who have become involved in offending. In Northern Ireland an adapted version of this tool is used. ASSET is a structured assessment tool that looks at the young person's offending and the factors that may have contributed to this behaviour. ASSET seeks to measure risk of reoffending and risk of harm based on research on risk factors for involvement in offending (Baker, 2008). The core components of the ASSET assessment are listed in Box 7.2.

Box 7.2   Core components of the ASSET assessment

- Offending behaviour
- Living arrangements
- Family and personal relationships
- Education, training and employment
- Neighbourhood
- Lifestyle
- Substance use
- Physical health
- Emotional and mental health
- Perception of self and others
- Thinking and behaviour
- Attitudes to offending
- Motivation to change
- Positive factors
- Indicators of vulnerability
- Indicators of serious harm to others

The ASSET assessment is used to measure the risk of reoffending and risk of harm and to therefore guide the nature of the intervention proposed to the court and undertaken with the young person. As in the adult criminal justice system, the direction of intervention in the youth justice system is orientated by risk. In many cases also, the range of interventions applicable to young people, in terms of court-ordered supervision, while bearing different names, has a striking similarity to adult orders and, in fact, some community-based sanctions available for young people are more intensive than anything similar for adults. One example of this are *intensive supervision and surveillance programmes*, which, in some contexts, require a young person to engage in supervised activities, observe curfews and comply with the directions of the youth justice worker. Part of the stated rationale for such intensive and intrusive programmes is they should be directed towards young people involved in prolific offending (Gray *et al.*, 2005). However, evidence also suggests that the imposition of certain sentences on young people is used as a means to address welfare needs that could or should have been met within the welfare system (Goldson, 2000b; Muncie, 2009).

A wider picture? Regional variation and local context

Variation within the UK in respect of youth justice systems is marked. As previously mentioned, Scotland's youth justice system is quite distinct with its particular emphasis on the welfare needs of the young person through the operation of the 'Hearing System'.

Scotland's 'Children's Hearing System'

The *Children's Hearing System* was introduced in Scotland following the passage of the *Social Work (Scotland) Act, 1968*. This legislation implemented the recommendations of the *Report of the Kilbrandon Commmittee* (SHHD, 1964, 1995), abolishing youth courts and establishing lay decision-making panels. One of the unique features of these panels, which comprise of lay members, is that they deal with both cases of juvenile offending and those children in need of care and protection (McGhee, 2011). The system is 'non-adversarial', which means that unlike the traditional court system they are not necessarily concerned with apportioning blame but rather with dealing with cases in the 'best interests of the child'. This 'welfare' principle is one of the key hallmarks of the *Children's Hearing System.*

There have been some key changes to the system since its introduction. Following the ratification of the *United Nations Convention on the Rights of the Child (UNCRC)*, the *Children (Scotland) Act, 1995* emphasised the importance of children's participation in the system. Article 12 of the UNCRC states that children should have the opportunity to be heard in any judicial or administrative proceedings affecting them. More recently the passage of the *Children's Hearings (Scotland) Act, 2011* has provided an updated framework for the system. Following from previous amendments, it outlines that the 'best interest' principle can be foregone in the interests of preventing serious harm.

What this means in practice is that in cases of serious offending the panel does not have to place the 'best interest' of the young person as its primary consideration. So, for example, it may be argued that it is not in the best interest of an individual young person to be detained in a secure unit, although this can be justified on the basis that the young person's detention is likely to prevent any further serious harm from offending. Examples such as this underline the complexity of decision-making and administration of youth justice systems, even within the 'welfarist' parameters of the *Children's Hearing System.*

Restorative justice in Northern Ireland

The youth justice system in Northern Ireland is also distinct, with the restorative justice model of 'youth conferencing' as the main disposal used within this system. Additionally the numbers of young people in custody in Northern Ireland have declined in relative terms in the same period that saw an expansion in the youth custody population in England and Wales. The reasons for such variation are invariably complex (Muncie, 2002; Muncie & Goldson, 2006; Whyte, 2010).

Northern Ireland also has a distinct criminal justice system that has been influenced by its particular social, historical and cultural context. In Northern Ireland the context of the *Troubles*, the 30-year-long civil conflict in which 3,000 people were killed, and the subsequent peace process, which included a commitment to critically review the criminal justice system, has been influential.

The *Criminal Justice Review (2000)* surveyed all aspects of the criminal justice system, including prosecution, court processes and sentencing, and recommended the formalisation of 'restorative justice' principles into the youth justice system through the implementation of legislation. This recommendation came as a result of the work of community-based restorative justice initiatives, which had been established as local projects to address offending, particularly where young people were under paramilitary threat as a result of alleged behaviour (Mika, 2006).

Restorative justice measures are now the primary disposal of the youth justice system in Northern Ireland. Such approaches are premised on the understanding that crime causes harm and restoration should focus on repairing the harm done (Zehr, 1990). A range of literature on restorative justice situates such approaches as the opposite of the more commonplace retributive model of justice.

The *Justice (NI) Act, 2002* led to the establishment of the *Youth Justice Agency*, an executive agency with an overall aim of youth crime reduction and with responsibility for the delivery of services in the youth justice system. The Act also led to the enactment of *youth conferencing orders*, a restorative justice disposal. Youth conferencing is the primary disposal of the Northern Ireland youth justice system. Youth conferences can take place at the pre-court stage as a diversionary measure on the recommendation of the Public Prosecution Service (PPS) or as a court-ordered measure.

A Youth Conference typically involves a meeting between the young person, the young person's parent or guardian, the victim of the offence (or a representative of the victim), a police officer and the youth conference coordinator. The meeting is intended as a 'restorative' intervention. This means that the young person should hear about the impact of the offence on the victim and acknowledge the harm caused. The outcome of the conference is the development of an Action Plan, which is agreed by all parties at the conference. Such a plan may include writing a letter of apology, undertaking voluntary work, agreeing to attend school etc. If the Conference is court-ordered the Action Plan is presented to court, and the court can then order that the young person fulfils the terms of the plan sentencing to a *Youth Conference Order*.

The legislation states that where a young person admits the offence a youth conference should take place (with the exception of certain serious offences). The use of restorative approaches within the criminal justice system broadly and within youth justice systems in particular has been the subject of positive endorsement, particularly when juxtaposed against the retributive justice model (Daly, 2002). There have been a number of positive evaluations of the Youth Conference approach (e.g. Campbell *et al.*, 2006; Maruna *et al.*, 2008), and there have been recent recommendations to extend the approach to other areas of the UK (Jacobson & Gibbs, 2006). However, some critics argue that restorative justice should ideally be community-led rather than formalised in a criminal justice system (Daly, 2002). Some observers also argue that restoration does not adequately address some of the underlying structural issues causing young people to engage in offending behaviour (Braithwaite, 1999). These debates are discussed more fully in Chapter 8.

The final section of this chapter considers the relevance of a children's rights perspective for the operation of the youth justice system.

Rights-based approaches

While there is undoubtedly evidence of *adulteration* of aspects of youth justice systems and practice, one of the key principles underpinning the rationale for separate justice systems for young people in various forms is recognition of the United Convention of the Rights of the Child (UNCRC), wherein a young person under 18 should be considered a child. The UNCRC is a universally ratified document and, in addition to the main convention, there are a number of non-binding treaties pertaining specifically to juvenile justice. These include standards on the 'Minimum Rules for the Administration of Juvenile Justice' (1985), guidelines on the prevention of delinquency and a set of rules relating to children who are deprived of their liberty.

The various rights-based instruments advocated principles such as diversion from formal processing in the criminal justice system and non-custodial measures. In fact, it is stated that custody should only be used as a 'measure of last resort'. The utility of rights-based approaches to young people involved in youth justice systems has been recognised. This is particularly underlined under Article 3 of the UNCRC, which states that, in all actions concerning children, the best interest of the child shall be a primary consideration. Various commentaries suggest that closer attention to a *rights-based* framework would lead to more positive outcomes for children and young people when they come into contact with systems of justice (Scraton & Haydon, 2002).

Conclusion

It will be evident that there is a range of rationales underpinning the operation of the youth justice system in the UK. Distinct and different systems of youth justice are in place in the various UK jurisdictions, and there is also variation in the age of criminal responsibility across the UK. However, there are also a number of themes that are similar in approaches to young people who come into conflict with the law. The question of whether approaches to young people should be welfare or justice oriented is the subject of ongoing debate, and shifts in perspectives and approaches are seen over time.

There is evidence of an increased punitive response to young people manifest in the introduction of Anti-Social Behaviour Orders and the general rise in custodial numbers. Also the use of risk factor analysis to determine the level and type of intervention has become an orthodox practice, both in the use of structured assessment tools and in the manner in which young people are viewed as 'risk' subjects who require management.

As a signatory to the UNCRC, the UK has committed to several basic principles, including diversion from the criminal justice system and the use of custody as a measure of last resort. Although the rise in the custodial population belies the latter commitment, it is argued that the application of a 'rights-based' framework could lead to more positive outcomes for young people.

Glossary

ASBOs (Anti-Social Behaviour Orders) – these are civil orders aimed at preventing behaviour that is 'likely to cause harm or distress'. A person subject to an ASBO can be subject to a range of prohibitions, for example, entry into a certain area or association with specific individuals. Breach of an ASBO can be prosecuted as a criminal offence.

ASSET – a structured risk assessment tool developed by the Youth Justice Board and used in practice in England and Wales. A version of this tool has been adapted for use in Northern Ireland also.

In camera **rule** – this rule means that proceedings in court involving children and young people should ordinarily be held in private (i.e. the public is not permitted to attend). It also means that the identities of children and young people should not be disclosed or published in media outlets. In some cases the court can decide to dispose of this rule of is deemed in the 'public interest'. This decision was taken in the court proceedings in the Bulger case and was subsequently roundly criticised.

Youth Conference Order – this order is available in courts in Northern Ireland. It is a restorative justice disposal, where following a *youth conference* an agreement is made between, the young person the injured party and representative of the community to undertake restoration for the offence. This plan is presented to the court and the court can then issue a Youth Conference Order in which the young person is sentenced to undertake the agreed plan.

Zahid Mubarek (1980–2000), aged 19 and a first-time offender, was killed by his cellmate in a racially motivated attack in Feltham Young Offender's Institution in 2000. The subsequent inquiry into his death strongly criticised a culture of racism within the prison service.

Source: Report of the Zahid Mubarek Inquiry (Crown Copyright)

Case Study

A Preventable Death

Figure 7.3 Zahid Mubarek

In 2000, Zahid Mubarek, an Asian teenager, was serving a short sentence at Feltham Young Offender Institution. He had not been to prison before. While there, he wrote movingly to his parents, admitting his shortcomings and expressing a determination not to let them down again. He was due to be released on 21 March.

But he was never to get the chance to prove that he had put his past behind him. In the early hours of that morning, he was brutally attacked by another young prisoner, Robert Stewart, with whom he had been sharing a cell for the previous six weeks. According to Stewart, Zahid had been asleep at the time, though some prisoners claimed to have heard screams. What is not in doubt is that Stewart clubbed him several times about the head with a wooden table leg. When help came, Zahid was barely conscious. Such was the ferocity of the attack that his father told the Inquiry that when he saw Zahid in hospital, "his head looked like a huge balloon. He was almost unrecognisable. His face was full of blood with bruising all over it." He died from his injuries a week later. He had been in a coma and never regained consciousness.

Some months before, Stewart had bragged about committing the first murder of the millennium. He was subsequently convicted of Zahid's murder. He was sentenced to life imprisonment. In convicting Stewart of murder, the jury rejected the suggestion that he should be convicted of manslaughter on the ground of diminished responsibility rather than murder.

Extract from the *Report of the Zahid Mubarek Inquiry*, Volume 1 (2006): xvii.

Seminar questions

1. Should children and young people be detained in prison environments?
2. At what age should children and young people be held criminally responsible for their actions?
3. What implications does a children's rights-based approach have for the youth justice system?

Further reading

Muncie, J. (2009) *Youth and Crime*, **3rd edn. London: Sage**
This book provides a comprehensive overview of some of the key debates and theories that inform youth justice policies and practices.

Scraton, P. (ed.) (2004) *Childhood in Crisis.* **London: Routledge**
Including contributions on a range of topics relating to children and young people, this text adopts a critical perspective to explore how intolerance towards young people impacts on policies and practice in a range of fora, including the youth justice system.

Taylor, W., Earle, R. & Hester, R. (eds) (2010) *Youth Justice Handbook: Theory, Policy and Practice.* **Cullompton: Willan Publishing**
This text includes up-to-date contributions on various aspects of youth justice practice with perspectives from different parts of the United Kingdom.

Further information can be obtained from the following websites

Youth Justice Board (England and Wales) – http://www.justice.gov.uk/about/yjb/

Youth Justice Agency (Northern Ireland) – http://www.youthjusticeagencyni.gov.uk/

Further information on the *Barnardo's 'Kids Inside'* campaign is available here: http://www.barnardos.org.uk/get_involved/campaign/kidsinside/about_kids_inside.htm

Further information on the *Edinburgh Youth Transitions Study,* including research reports and publications available here: http://www.law.ed.ac.uk/cls/esytc/

References

Ashworth, A., Gardner, J., Morgan, R., Smith, A., Von Hirsch, A. & Wasik, M. (1998) 'Neighbouring on the oppressive: The government's "Anti-Social Behaviour Order" proposals', *Criminal Justice*, 16, 1: 7–14

Baker, K. (2008) 'Risk, uncertainty and public protection: Assessment of young people who offend', *British Journal of Social Work*, 38, 8: 1463–80

Barnardos (2010) *From Playground to Prison: The Case for Reviewing the Age of Criminal Responsibility*. Ilford, Essex: Barnardo's

Bottoms, A. (1995) 'The philosophy and politics of punishment and sentencing'. In: C. Clarkson and R. Morgan (eds) *The Politics of Sentencing Reform*. Oxford: Clarendon Press, pp. 17–49

Braithwaite, J. (1999) 'Restorative justice: Assessing optimistic and pessimistic accounts', *Crime and Justice*, 25: 1–127

Campbell, C., Devlin, R., O'Mahoney, D., Doak, J., Jackson, J., Corrigan, T. & McEvoy, K. (2006) *Evaluation of the Northern Ireland Youth Conference Service*. Belfast: Northern Ireland Office

Campbell, S. (2002) *A Review of Anti-Social Behaviour Orders*. Home Office Research Study 236. London: Home Office Research and Statistics Directorate

Carlile Report (Lord Carlile of Berriew) (2006) *The Carlile Inquiry: An Independent Inquiry into the Use of Physical Restraint, Solitary Confinement and Forcible Strip Searching of Children in Prisons, Secure Training Centres and Local Authority Secure Children's Homes*. London: The Howard League

Coles, D. (2011) 'Teenagers' deaths in custody are needless', *Guardian*, 6 May 2011

Coles, D. & Goldson, B. (2005) *In the Care of the State? Child Deaths in Penal Custody*. London: Inquest

Commission for Racial Equality (CRE) (2003) *Race Equality in Prisons. A Formal Investigation by the Commission for Racial Equality into HM Prison Service of England and Wales, Part 2*. London: Commission for Racial Equality

Croall, H. (2006) 'Criminal justice policy in post-devolutionary Scotland', *Critical Social Policy*, 26, 3: 587–607

Daly, K. (2002) 'Restorative justice: the real story', *Punishment and Society*, 4, 1: 55–79

Doherty, K. (2010) 'The development of restorative justice in Northern Ireland'. In: W. Taylor, R. Earle & R. Hester (eds) *Youth Justice Handbook: Theory, Policy and Practice*. Cullompton: Willan Publishing, pp. 243–52

Farrington, D.P. (1989) 'Early predictors of adolescent aggression and violence', *Violence and Victims*, 4: 79–100

Farrington, D.P. (1995) 'The development of offending and anti-social behaviour from childhood: Key findings from the Cambridge Study in Delinquent Development', *Journal of Child Psychology and Psychiatry*, 36: 929–64

Farrington, D.P. (2000) 'Explaining and preventing crime: The globalization of knowledge', *Criminology*, 38, 1: 1–24

Farrington, D.P. (2007) 'Childhood risk factors and risk-focused prevention'. In: M. Maguire, R. Morgan & R. Reiner (eds) *The Oxford Handbook of Criminology*. Oxford: Oxford University Press

Feilzer, M. & Hood, R. (2004) *Differences or Discrimination?* London: Youth Justice Board

Fergusson, D.M., Horwood, L.J. & Lynskey, M.T. (1993) 'The effects of conduct disorder and attention deficit in middle childhood on offending and scholastic ability at age 13', *Journal of Child Psychology and Psychiatry*, 34: 899–916

France, A. & Crow, I. (2005) 'Using the "Risk Factor Paradigm" in prevention: Lessons from the evaluation of Communities that Care', *Children and Society*, 19: 172–84

Garland, D. (2001) *Culture of Control: Crime and Social Order in Contemporary Society*. Oxford: Oxford University Press

Goldson, B. (2000a) 'Whither diversion? Interventionism and the new youth justice'. In: B. Goldson (ed.) *The New Youth Justice.* Lyme Regis: Russell House

Goldson, B. (2000b) 'Children in need or young offenders?,' *Child and Family Social Work,* 5, 3: 255–65

Goldson, B. (2002) 'New punitiveness: The politics of child incarceration'. In: J. Muncie, G. Hughes & E. McLaughlin (eds) *Youth Justice: Critical Readings.* London: Sage

Gray, P. (2005) 'The politics of risk and young offenders' experiences of social exclusion and restorative justice', *British Journal of Criminology,* 45, 6: 938–57

Haines, K. & Case, S. (2008) 'The rhetoric and reality of the "Risk Factor Prevention Paradigm" approach to preventing and reducing offending', *Youth Justice,* 8, 1: 5–20

Haydon, D. & Scraton, P. (2000) "Condemn a little more, understand a little less": The political context and rights' implications of the domestic and European rulings in the Venables–Thompson case', *Journal of Law and Society,* 27, 3: 416–48

Homel, R. (2005) 'Developmental crime prevention'. In: N. Tilley (ed.) *Handbook of Crime Prevention and Community Safety.* Cullompton: Willan Publishing

Huizinga, D., Schumann, K., Ehret, B. & Elliot, A. (2003) *The Effects of Juvenile Justice Processing on Subsequent Delinquent and Criminal Behaviour: A Cross-National Study.* Washington, DC: Final Report to the National Institute of Justice

Jacobson, J. & Gibbs, P. (2009) *Out of Trouble. Making Amends: Restorative Justice in Northern Ireland.* London: Prison Reform Trust

Keith, B. (2006) *Report of the Zahid Mubarek Inquiry, Vols 1 and 2.* London: The Stationery Office

Kilbrandon, Lord (1966) 'Children in trouble with the law', *British Journal of Criminology,* 6, 2: 112–22

Mackie, A., Hubbard, R. & Burrows, J. (2008) *Evaluation of the Youth Inclusion Programme, Phase 2.* London: Youth Justice Board

McAra, L. & McVie, S. (2007) 'Youth justice? The impact of system contact on patterns of desistance from offending', *European Journal of Criminology,* 4, 3: 315–45

McGhee, J. (2011) 'Children's Hearings in Scotland: Balancing rights and welfare'. In: R. Davis & J. Gordon (eds) *Social Work and the Law in Scotland.* Basingstoke: Palgrave Macmillan

Maruna, S., Wright, S., Brown, J., van Merle, F., Devlin, R. and Liddle, M. (2007) Youth Conferencing as Shame Management: Results of a long-term follow-up study. Cambridge: ARCS (UK) Ltd.

Mika, H. (2006) *Community-based Restorative Justice Initiatives in Northern Ireland.* Belfast: Queen's University Belfast

Muncie, J. (1999) 'Institutionalised intolerance: Youth justice and the 1998 Crime and Disorder Act', *Critical Social Policy,* 19, 2: 147–75

Muncie, J. (2002) 'Policy transfers and what works: Some reflections on comparative youth justice', *Youth Justice,* 1, 3: 27–35

Muncie, J. (2005) 'The globalisation of crime control: The case of youth and juvenile justice', *Theoretical Criminology,* 9, 1: 35–64

Muncie, J. (2006) 'Governing young people: Coherence and contradiction in contemporary youth justice'. *Critical Social Policy,* 26, 4: 770–93

Muncie, J. (2008) 'The punitive turn in juvenile justice: Cultures of control and rights compliance in western Europe and the USA', *Youth Justice: An International Journal,* 8, 2: 107–21

Muncie, J. (2009) *Youth and Crime,* 3rd edn. London: Sage

Muncie, J. & Goldson, B. (2006) *Comparative Youth Justice.* London: Sage

Newburn, T. (2002) 'The contemporary politics of youth crime prevention'. In: J. Muncie, G. Hughes & E. McLaughlin (eds) *Youth Justice: Critical Readings*. London: Sage, pp. 452–64

O'Mahony, P. (2009) 'The risk factors prevention paradigm and the causes of youth crime: A deceptively useful analysis?,' *Youth Justice*, 9, 2: 99–114

Paylor, I. (2011) 'Youth justice in England and Wales: A risky business', *Journal of Offender Rehabilitation*, 50, 4: 221–33

Scraton, P. (ed.) (1997) *Childhood in Crisis*. London: UCL Press

Scraton, P. and Haydon, D. (2002) 'Challenging the Criminalization of Children and Young People: Securing a Rights-based Agenda', in J. Muncie, G. Hughes and E. McLaughlin (eds) *Youth Justice: Critical Readings*. London: SAGE, pp. 311–28.

Sherman, L., Gottfredson, D., MacKenzie, D., Eck, J., Reuter, P. & Bushway, S. (1998) *Preventing Crime: What Works, What Doesn't, What's Promising*. Baltimore: University of Maryland, Department of Criminology and Criminal Justice

Smith, D.J. (2006) *Social Inclusion and Early Desistance from Crime. Edinburgh Study of Youth Transitions and Crime*. Research Digest No. 12.

Smith, D. & McAra, L. (2004) *Gender and Youth Offending*. Edinburgh: University of Edinburgh

Smith, D. and McVie, S. (2003) 'Theory and method in the Edinburgh Study of Youth Transitions and Crime', *British Journal of Criminology*, 43, 1: 169–95

Squires, P. & Stephen, D. (2005) 'Rethinking ASBOs', *Critical Social Policy*, 25, 4: 517–28

Thomas, M., Vuong, K. & Renshaw, J. (2004) 'ASBOs target youths, but to what effect?', *Safer Society*, 23 (Winter): 25–6.

Tisdall, K. (2006) 'Antisocial behaviour legislation meets children's services: Challenging perspectives on children, parents and the state', *Critical Social Policy*, 26, 1: 101–20

Tracy, P.E. & Kempf-Leonard, K. (1996) *Continuity and Discontinuity in Criminal Careers*. New York: Plenum

Ward, T. & Maruna, S. (2007) *Rehabilitation*. London: Routledge

Webster, C., MacDonald, R. & Simpson, M. (2006) 'Predicting criminality? Risk factors, neighbourhood influence and desistance', *Youth Justice*, 6, 1: 7–22

West, D.J. & Farrington, D.P. (1973) *Who Becomes Delinquent?* London: Heinemann

Whyte, B. (2009) *Youth Justice in Practice: Making a Difference*. Bristol: Policy Press

Whyte, B. (2010) 'Values in youth justice: Practice approaches to welfare and justice for young people in UK jurisdictions'. In: W. Taylor, R. Earle & R. Hester (eds) *Youth Justice Handbook: Theory, Policy and Practice*. Cullompton: Willan Publishing, pp. 221–31

Wikstrom, P.O. (1998) *Patterns of Crime in a Birth Cohort*. Stockholm: University of Stockholm

Wikstrom, T. & Loeber, R. (1998) 'Individual risk factors, neighbourhood SES and juvenile offending'. In: M. Tonry (ed.) *The Handbook of Crime and Punishment*. New York: Oxford University Press

Youth Justice Board (YJB) (2005) *Role of Risk and Protective Factors*. London: YJB

Zehr, H. (1990) *Changing Lenses: A New Focus for Crime and Justice*. Scottdale, PA: Herald Press.

8 Restorative justice

An alternative mode of justice?

Key issues

- What is restorative justice?
- How is restorative justice practiced in the UK?
- Can restorative approaches offer an alternative model of justice?

Introduction

So far in this book we have focused on how individuals who are charged, prosecuted and sentenced for offences are processed through the criminal justice system. We have highlighted that the criminal justice system in the various parts of the United Kingdom operates an *adversarial model* of justice. This is particularly evident in the forum of the court, where the prosecution must prove beyond reasonable doubt that the alleged perpetrator committed the offence. And although an offence may directly involve a victim, for example, in the case of an assault, it is the State or the Crown, through its representatives, the prosecution agencies, who prosecute the offences. This reflects the fact that in effect that it is the sovereign who has been offended against by the commission of an offence in her territory. In this sense the victim is displaced. Christie (1977), who describes crime as a conflict, which has been appropriated from the parties involved by the State, observes the following:

> the one party that is represented by the state, namely the victim, is so thoroughly represented that she or he for the most part of the proceedings is pushed completely out of the scene, reduced to the triggerer-off of the whole thing. She or he is sort of a double loser; first vis-à-vis the offender, but secondly and often in a more crippling manner by being denied rights to full participation in what might have been one of the more important ritual encounters in life. The victim has lost the case to the state.
>
> (Christie, 1977: 3)

Here Christie (1977) argues that the conflict between the parties involved is taken over by the State and as such several things are lost, including the possibility of the victim making the offender aware of the harm that has been caused and the opportunity for the wider community to reassert its norms. Of course, the appropriation of the 'conflict' by the State also has benefits. Firstly, it is arguably the case that the criminal justice system is a central pillar in maintaining social order. What sort of society would we have if individuals were left to solve their own conflicts? Secondly, the State prosecuting the offender rather than the victim potentially protects the victims, who may not wish to have to resolve the conflict themselves, even if it was in their power to do so.

Nonetheless, the argument that the victim of crime has been sidelined and that the criminal justice system is not effective in meeting the needs of victims is a persuasive one. The question of how victims can be more properly served by the criminal justice system has become a central question in recent years (Davies *et al.*, 2007). This has been linked in part to rights-based victims' movements, which have demanded a more victim-oriented criminal justice system. *Victim Support*, established in the UK in 1974, is the most prominent victims-rights movement in the UK. Now a national charity operational in all regions of the UK, *Victim Support* campaigns and advocates on behalf of victims of crime. It also provides confidential help to victims (and witnesses) of crime who can contact the organisation directly.

In a report for *Victim Support*, Cory (2011) identifies that victims of crime remain largely dissatisfied with the criminal justice system. This relates to all stages of the criminal justice process, including the decision to report a crime in the first instance. As discussed in Chapter 1, numerous studies reveal that official data on crime obtained from police records represents only a small proportion of all crime committed.

While increased attention has been paid to victims and their treatment within the criminal justice system in recent years, more critical commentators have questioned the real impact of these measures on victims' experiences of the criminal justice system and process (Edwards, 2004). Indeed, some argue that the retributive and adversarial model of justice that operates in the United Kingdom is particularly unsuited to meeting the needs of victims to any satisfactory degree and that this represents a fundamental difficulty that cannot be addressed by initiatives such as those described. In this context, it has been argued that a *restorative justice* model offers a more satisfactory and meaningful engagement for victims of crime, and proponents argue that it is ultimately more effective in reducing offending as one if its central aims is to encourage offenders to confront the reality of the harm caused (Dignan, 2007; Morris, 2002).

The following section of this chapter provides a brief overview of the evolution of restorative justice approaches within the UK. The main principles of restorative justice and some of the theories underpinning this approach are defined.

Restorative justice – a short history

Most accounts tracing the origin of restorative justice approaches note antecedents from conflict-resolution and victim-centred approaches in Maori, Aboriginal and Native American culture (Johnstone, 2003). Other scholars have also pointed towards traditions closer to home that pre-dated our more formalised approaches to criminal justice (Consedine, 1995).

In New Zealand and Australia the formal criminal justice system adopted restorative justice approaches in the 1980s and 1990s, partly in response to the over-representation of young people from indigenous minority groups in the criminal justice system. The example of the introduction of a youth conferencing approach (a restorative justice intervention) in the city of Wagga Wagga in New South Wales is frequently cited (Liebmann, 2007). In Wagga Wagga police instigated an initiative to respond to crime that involved a meeting between the victim, perpetrator and community representatives in order to explore the impact of the crime on all parties and work towards reparation and resolution.

'Reintegrative shaming' is one of the key concepts underpinning restorative justice approaches (Braithwaite, 1989). The term, coined by Braithwaite (1989), refers to the importance of shame for the perpetrator in understanding the harm caused by their actions. However, the concept of *reintegration* is also key. It is argued that our conventional criminal justice system, the adversarial model we have described in the preceding chapters, is one that is overly focused on punishment and exclusion – most evident in the use of imprisonment – but not sufficiently focused on the offender's reintegration into the community when punishment has been served.

The reason why reintegration is important, not just in moral terms, is that people who feel that they are part of their communities and have a stake in society may be less likely to commit further offences. This perspective accords with social control theories, which contend that people's relationships, social norms, beliefs and values are important factors in whether people break the law. Hirschi (1969) argued that stronger social controls meant that offending was less likely. This is also reflected in the literature on *desistance,* as discussed in Chapter 5, that is, the reasons why people stop offending are partly related to the strength of social bonds.

The perspectives offered by *labelling theory* also help us to understand why the stigmatisation and exclusion of the perpetrator of crime may ultimately be counter-productive (Becker, 1963; Erikson, 1962). Labelling theorists argue that the processing of people through the criminal justice system and the categorisation of people as offenders leads to a negative self-identification that is itself *criminogenic,* that is, linked with further offending. Indeed, as discussed in the previous chapter, this perspective has been taken on board in initiatives focusing on young people in particular where *diversion* from the formal criminal justice system is seen to be more effective than processing people through it (McAra & McVie, 2007).

A third key perspective that supports the use of restorative justice approaches concerns the perspective of victims of offences. Here, as Christie (1977) and others have persuasively argued, the victim is sidelined in adversarial criminal justice proceedings (Hoyle & Zedner, 2007). The victim's concerns and experiences are expressed through the words of others in a highly formalised and rule-bound process. Research on the experiences of victims within the conventional criminal justice system also frequently points to highly negative experiences, including feelings of not being believed and encounters that cause retraumatisation. For example, a recent evaluation of young people's experiences as victims and witnesses in the criminal justice system in Northern Ireland highlights that young people may be subjected to intrusive cross-examination in the witness box and feel that they are being undermined (Hayes *et al.*, 2011). This is despite the fact that so-called *special measures* have been put in place for young and vulnerable witnesses (see Box 8.1).

Box 8.1   Special measures available for vulnerable and intimidated witnesses

In recognition of the particular difficulties in giving evidence and being cross-examined in an adversarial court process a range of 'special measures' are available for victims and witnesses who are deemed to be vulnerable or who may face intimidation. In England and Wales the *Youth Justice and Criminal Evidence Act (1999)* defines who is eligible for these 'special measures':

- Children are defined as vulnerable by reason of age;
- Witnesses who have a mental disorder as detailed under the Mental Health Act 1983;
- Witnesses significantly impaired in relation to intelligence and social functioning; and
- Physically disabled witnesses.

The type of measures available are:

Screens, (available for all vulnerable and intimidated witnesses): screens may be made available to shield the witness from the defendant

Live link, (available for all vulnerable and intimidated witnesses): the live link will enable the witness to give evidence during the trial from outside the court through a televised link to the courtroom. The witness may be accommodated either within the court building or in a suitable location outside the court

---

Evidence given in private, (available for all vulnerable and intimidated witnesses): exclusion from the court of members of the public and the press (except for one named person to represent the press) will be considered in cases involving sexual offences or intimidation

Removal of wigs and gowns, (available for all vulnerable and intimidated witnesses at the Crown Court): removal of wigs and gowns by judges and barristers

Examination of the witness through an intermediary: an intermediary may be appointed by the court to assist the witness to give their evidence at court. This measure is only available to vulnerable witnesses

Aids to communication, (available for vulnerable witnesses): aids to communication will be permitted to enable the witness to give best evidence whether through a communicator or interpreter, or through a communication aid or technique, provided that the communication can be independently verified and understood by the court. This measure is only available to vulnerable witnesses

So one of the questions posed in this chapter is whether *restorative justice* offers an alternative way of thinking about justice for those most affected by crime. Implicit in the term *restorative justice* is the concept of 'restoration' – that is, to restore the harm caused by the act of an offence. Here it is recognised that harm is caused to all parties involved in the offence and that the purpose of justice should be to focus on recognising this fact and on repairing this harm. The principles of restorative justice processes set out in Box 8.2 attest to the aims of this form of justice.

Box 8.2 Restorative justice processes

1. Primary aim to be the repair of harm.
2. Agreement about essential facts of the incident and an acceptance of some involvement by the person who caused the harm.
3. Participation to be voluntary for all participants and based on an informed choice. This also applies to what is included in any outcome agreement, and any consequence for non-participation/compliance to be made clear.
4. Adequate time to be given to participants to decide whether to take part and to consult with others, if they wish.

5. Acknowledgment of harm or loss experienced by the persons harmed, respect for the feelings of participants, and an opportunity for the resulting needs to be considered and where possible met.
6. The person/s who have been harmed or suffered loss to be (if they wish) the primary beneficiary of any reparation agreed with the person who has caused the harm.
7. Where harm is repaired or amends made, this to be acknowledged and valued.
8. The person/s who has harmed and the person/s harmed are the primary participants in the restorative process.
9. Restorative practitioners to be seen as neutral by participants, and to act impartially.

Source: Restorative Justice Consortium: Principles of Restorative Processes (2004).

Restorative justice approaches

In 2002 the *United Nations* produced the following definition of the restorative process:

> 'Restorative process' means any process in which the victim and the offender, and where appropriate, any other individuals or community members affected by a crime participate together actively in the resolution of matters arising from the crime, generally with the help of a facilitator. Restorative approaches may include mediation, conciliation, conferencing and sentencing circles.
>
> (United Nations: *Basic Principles on the use of Restorative Justice Programmes in Criminal Matters* (2002))[1]

This definition points to the fact that a broad range of interventions can be included under the remit of restorative justice. At its simplest level restorative justice can involve a facilitated meeting between the victim, offender and a representative of the community, in which there is a dialogue between the participants. The purpose of this dialogue is to allow the victim to articulate the harm caused by the offence and to enable the offender to take responsibility for the harm done. One of the desired outcomes of such an approach is that the offender commits to do something to 'restore' or put right the harm. This could involve making a commitment to undertake unpaid work, writing a letter of apology, paying compensation to the victim or engaging in a specific programme to address the causes of offending (Dignan, 2007).

Bearing in mind the critiques of conventional models of justice, proponents of restorative justice argue that restorative approaches allow for a more meaningful engagement for all parties. As Morris (2002: 598) notes, restorative justice also emphasises human rights and the need to recognise the impact of social or substantive injustice and in small ways address these rather than simply provide offenders with legal or formal justice and victims with no justice at all. Thus it seeks to restore the victim's security, self-respect, dignity and, most importantly, sense of control. And it seeks to restore responsibility to offenders for their offending and its consequences, to restore a sense of control to them to make amends for what they have done and to restore a belief in them that the process and outcomes were fair and just.

Restorative justice approaches are associated with a broad range of processes – a list of some common examples is provided in Box 8.3. What characterises the interventions as being *restorative* is their adherence to the principles already described. However, it must be noted that the experience of restorative justice is context-dependent and very much influenced by the dynamic of the process, issues that we discuss later in this chapter.

Box 8.3   Some common restorative justice processes

Victim–Offender Mediation: This involves a meeting between the victim and the offender, which is facilitated by a trained person. The mediator is an impartial third party who helps to facilitate the meeting. The idea is to assist the victim and offender to exchange information, ideas and emotions and to build a mutual understanding of the events and of each other as human beings. Once the parties are satisfied that they have had their say, the facilitator helps the parties think through options for making things right.

Restorative Circles
Circles are facilitated community meetings attended by offenders, victims, their friends and families, interested members of the community, and (usually) representatives of the justice system. The facilitator is a community member (called a 'keeper') whose role is primarily to keep the process orderly and periodically to summarize for the benefit of the circle. They are derived from aboriginal peacemaking practices in North America.

Restorative Conferencing
Conferencing brings the victim and offender to a face-to-face meeting to discuss the crime and its impact. This process includes support people for

---

both the victim and offender in the discussions. Representatives from the criminal justice system may also be present in the conference process. A trained facilitator, who does not have a role in the substantive discussions, guides the participants in a dialogue about the crime and its impact. The facilitator ensures that each participant has a voice in the proceedings.

Source: Restorative Justice Online
http://www.restorativejustice.org/press-room/05rjprocesses

Restorative justice in the criminal justice continuum

The use of restorative approaches has gained increasing currency and popularity in recent years, and the types of interventions and the stages within the criminal justice system at which they occur vary across the United Kingdom. In some instances restorative measures are used as an alternative to processing cases through the criminal justice system. However, this tends to be for relatively low-level offending, and the circumstances in which this can be used are usually strictly proscribed. Thames Valley Police were one of the first police forces in the United Kingdom to adopt a restorative approach towards administering police cautions. This involved police officers inviting all those affected by an offence to participate in a restorative meeting. The evaluation of the initiative found that participants (offenders, victims and other involved parties) were generally positive about the experience. Importantly, it supports the claim that restorative justice was more effective than the more traditional approach (which some described as the equivalent of receiving a 'bollocking' from a police officer) in reducing reoffending (Hoyle *et al.*, 2002).

In other instances restorative justice approaches are used as a diversionary measure at the pre-court stage. Here in some contexts the prosecution agency can redirect the case towards a restorative measure rather than proceeding to court. This option is obviously dependent on the availability of such schemes, and for all of these approaches the offender must admit guilt before being eligible for referral. Restorative initiatives have also been used at pre-sentence and post-conviction stages at several sites throughout the UK. A study by Shapland and associates (2006) has explored the implementation and outcome of some of these initiatives across England, again with broadly positive results in terms of participants' experience of the process. Restorative approaches have also been used in later phases of the criminal justice process, for example, with people on probation or in prison following sentence.

Broadly speaking, while restorative approaches have been generally positively received they have tended to be implemented in the UK context as adjuncts to existing criminal justice processes. However, in the Northern Ireland context the evolution of restorative justice has been somewhat different, originating as a response to a legitimacy deficit in local communities. The following section of the chapter describes the origins and context of restorative justice within Northern Ireland.

Northern Ireland

In Northern Ireland the use of restorative justice approaches both within local communities and as a more formal element of the criminal justice system has been closely entwined in the transition from conflict of this society (Eriksson, 2009; McEvoy & Mika, 2002). Restorative justice approaches initially emerged in local communities in response to and as an alternative to paramilitary violence, in particular to so-called 'punishment beatings' and shootings meted out to community members who were involved in undesired behaviour (e.g. alleged drug use and criminality) (Eriksson, 2009; Knox, 2001). It is argued that part of the reason for *paramilitary policing* of local communities was a response to the absence of a legitimate criminal justice response. And indeed the *Patten Report* (1999) on policing reform in Northern Ireland recognised the significant difficulties related to policing. Consequently, the report recommended replacing the Royal Ulster Constabulary (RUC) with a new police force, the Police Service for Northern Ireland (PSNI) (*Patten Report, 1999*).

As McEvoy and Mika (2002) highlight, community-based restorative justice projects:

> were established in large part to facilitate paramilitaries moving away from violence punishment systems developed over the past three decades. Community-based restorative justice projects were designed to allow such paramilitaries to (in their terms) 'disengage responsibly' from such acts, handing dispute resolution back to local communities from which the conflicts emanate.
>
> (McEvoy & Mika, 2002: 535)

These projects were established in some Republican and Loyalist areas with the support of the Northern Ireland Association for the Care and Rehabilitation of Offenders (NIACRO). The *Criminal Justice Review* (2000), an overarching review of the criminal justice system in Northern Ireland conducted as part of the peace process, acknowledged the role that community-based restorative justice initiatives played in dealing with 'low-level' crime in local communities. The review also recommended the adoption of restorative justice approaches within the youth justice system. This led to the introduction of legislation, which set out that a restorative justice approach: youth justice conferences were to be the primary method for dealing with young people in the criminal justice system.[2]

The *Youth Justice Agency*, established as an executive agency in 2003, has responsibility for the operation of the youth conferencing service within Northern Ireland. There are two types of youth conferences: diversionary and court-ordered. The Public Prosecution Service can refer a child or young person to the Youth Justice Agency for a youth justice conference as an alternative to prosecution (diversionary), and the court can refer the child or young person for a conference (court-ordered). A number of eligibility criteria apply, central to which is that the young person must admit to the offence and agree to participate in the conference. If these and other criteria are not met, the case will proceed through the normal prosecution routes (Doherty, 2010).

The youth conference is a restorative justice meeting between the young person, an appropriate adult, the victim of the offence (or a representative), a youth conference coordinator who chairs the meeting and a police officer. The intended outcome of the meeting is a *youth conference plan*, which may involve (but is not limited to) any of the following: an apology to the victim; reparation to the victim or the community; engagement in unpaid work or participation in specific activities, for example, education and training. The intention of the youth justice conference is that all parties will be heard and will agree on the conference plan. For court-ordered conferences, the plan is then submitted to court, and the court can choose to make amendments before issuing a *youth conference order*. In the case of diversionary conferences the plan is submitted to the Public Prosecution Service (Doherty, 2010).

A number of evaluations have been conducted on youth conferencing (e.g. Campbell *et al.*, 2005; Maruna *et al.*, 2007). These highlight a number of issues. Firstly, victims who participated reported a high level of satisfaction with the process (Campbell *et al.*, 2005), and many young people commented that the experience was less daunting than they had anticipated and certainly preferable to more formal proceedings (Maruna *et al.*, 2007). However, it has also been noted that some participants had negative experiences of the process. For example, there is currently no limit on the number of conferences that a young person can have, therefore some young people attended multiple conferences with little discernible impact. Secondly, in the research conducted by Maruna *et al.* (2007) some young people reported the negative experience of feeling that they were being 'lectured' at, rather than being involved in a truly restorative process.

While the Northern Irish youth conference model is one example of an attempt to integrate a restorative justice approach into the mainstream criminal/youth justice system, there are criticisms made of what has been characterised as the co-option of what was originally intended as a community-based justice model by the State (McAlister *et al.*, 2009; McEvoy & Mika, 2002). It is argued that the community is a central stakeholder in the restorative justice context, both in terms of signifying disapproval of the offending, but also in terms of rein-tegration, as the concept of reintegrative shaming implies. Critics of State-led restorative justice approaches therefore argue that the community becomes lost in such initiatives.

This is precisely the criticism that has been made in respect of community-based restorative justice initiatives and the attempts that have been made by the State to regulate them. In 2007 the Northern Ireland Office issued a protocol, which aimed to set out the parameters of interaction between community-based schemes and the formal criminal justice system.[3] It specified the following:

> This Protocol applies to all cases where schemes deal or seek to deal with criminal offences. All such cases must be passed via the police to the Public Prosecution Service, who will refer suitable low-level offences back to schemes to be dealt with in accordance with the Protocol. Schemes must not deal with more serious offences, including e.g. sexual offences or cases of domestic violence, or any criminal offences not the subject of a referral from the Public Prosecution Service.
>
> (NIO, 2007: 1)

Some proponents argue that these types of measures are reflective of the State reasserting its authority over the realm of criminal justice. On the other hand, some would observe that the issuing of protocols and standards of practice are aimed to ensure the proper safeguards are in place in the administration of justice (Criminal Justice Inspection Northern Ireland, 2009). Whatever the reality of these two viewpoints, the issues raised in the Northern Ireland context speak to broader critiques of restorative justice approaches, which the next section of this chapter will address.

Critiques of restorative justice

Critiques of restorative justice models include arguments made by 'just deserts' proponents that the sanction imposed does not necessarily fit the crime, thereby leading to inequities in the administration of justice (Ashworth, 2002; Ashworth & von Hirsch, 1998). Further questions in relation to due process have been raised, particularly given that the offender must be prepared to admit to the crime before engagement in a restorative justice intervention. Analysts of restorative justice approaches in the context of the youth justice system argue that there may be an in-built incentive for young people to admit to crimes they have not committed in order to engage in a restorative justice intervention rather than face a potentially more daunting court process (Hudson, 2002).

Further some critics have argued that restorative justice approaches are inappropriate for particular types of crime, including domestic violence, sexual assault and hate crimes (Daly, 2002). Here it is argued that a restorative justice response does not adequately protect victims of crime or indicate the seriousness of such crimes in the manner in which the 'formal' criminal justice system is intended to do.

As a response to this, however, Hudson (2002) points out that the formal criminal justice system has not proven very successful in dealing with these types of crimes – evident in the previously described pattern of low reporting and low conviction rates for such crimes.

Morris (2002) further contends that critiques of restorative justice are often based on fundamental misunderstandings of what restorative justice seeks to achieve and/or on misinterpretation of empirical research on restorative justice. In any event, Morris (2002) goes on to argue that criticisms of restorative justice should not just be based on a comparison with retributive models of justice as this can lead to a potential false dichotomy.

Conclusion

The concept of restorative approaches to justice has gained increasing currency in various contexts within the criminal justice system in recent years. In part this is reflective of an overall dissatisfaction of victims and other parties involved with the highly proceduralised and adversarial approach that is characteristic of our current criminal justice system and which the previous chapters of this book have sought to critically interrogate. The attraction of restorative justice is also reflective of a *realpolitik* – a realisation that conventional approaches have not proven particularly effective in reducing offending, the use of imprisonment being the most obvious example. Notwithstanding the attractiveness of the idea of restorative justice and indeed what has been described as the 'seductiveness' of this approach (Maruna, 2011), legitimate concerns have been raised about what restorative justice means in practice. Some of these critiques can be encapsulated in the following two rhetorical questions: Restored to what? Restored to whom?

Indeed, some of the most vociferous critiques of this alternative model of justice have noted the manner in which restorative justice has been added on to conventional systems – the argument here is: so what's the difference? Having considered this question, it is worth returning to Alison Morris's (2002) point – that an adversarial and retributive system has not served us well, therefore alternative models of justice should not simply be criticised on the basis that it has not realised what other approaches have also failed to deliver. What we can look towards is a range of research that notes that restorative justice, when implemented properly, and where restoration does occur, can bring about positive change for the victim, offender and the community.

Glossary

Reintegrative shaming – is a term used to note the importance of the process of shame in recognising wrongdoing. It also pays attention to the importance of reintegration – that is, the opposite of exclusionary approaches.

Restorative justice processes – a range of principles and approaches that involve the parties in an offence in an aim to recognise and redress the harm caused by the offence.

Special measures – are a range of adaptations or measures that can be implemented on request in the court setting for vulnerable and/or intimidated witnesses.

Victim–Offender mediation – associated with the restorative justice approach, Victim–Offender mediation typically involves a meeting between the victim and the offender, which is facilitated by a trained person. The mediator is an impartial third party who helps to facilitate the meeting.

Case study

Meeting our son's killer

It was after midnight when Ray and Vi Donovan's door bell rang. Ray got out of bed and went downstairs assuming his two sons, Chris and Phil, had forgotten their keys. When he opened the door Ray found two police officers who explained that his sons had been attacked by a gang of youths and they must come to the hospital straight away.

Whilst walking home Chris and his brother Phil saw a gang of boys and girls coming towards them. As they got nearer the gang opened up to let them pass, but as they were walking through the gang punched and pulled Chris and Phil to the ground. They kicked and stamped on Chris' head and then left him in the middle of the four-lane road. A car came over the hill and ran over Chris, dragging him about forty feet down the road.

The doctors told Ray and Vi that they were sorry, they had done all they could for Christopher. Before they could say anything further Vi ran out of the door. She said later she felt that if she ran away it wouldn't be real. Vi recalls her rage at the time and the feeling of wanting to find her son's killers and to 'do to them what they had done to Chris'. Ray remembers falling to his knees screaming. Three boys were arrested and found guilty of Chris's murder. Their ages were fifteen, sixteen and nineteen. During the court case Vi remembers the look of pain and shame etched on the faces of the boys' parents. 'You just realise that everyone is losing here. It will never be the same for any of us.'

Several years later, one of the young men that killed Chris contacted Ray and Vi saying that he would like to meet and say sorry. At the time Ray and Vi were told by Probation that the meeting could not happen, but were allowed to send all three a letter telling the young men that they were forgiven and that they hoped that one day they would be able to meet and talk.

Years later still Ray and Vi came into contact with CALM (Confidential and Local Mediation), an RJC member providing restorative justice in areas of North London. With the help of CALM, Ray and Vi contacted the men and all said that they wanted to meet. Over the next few months CALM helped Ray and Vi prepare for the meeting and ensured the men were genuinely ready to face them.

Finally the day came for Ray and Vi to meet one of the young men that killed Chris. They had many questions which he was able to answer. In particular they wanted to know how he could have left Chris in the middle of a busy road. He told them how he had heard sirens and thought the police were coming so ran away. He said that he had been a fifteen year old coward and that now he couldn't get Chris out of his heart.

Ray has said: 'My wife and I left that meeting feeling like a weight had been lifted. We know that without the help of restorative justice this would never have happened. Restorative justice gives the victim a voice and helps the perpetrator of harm to think about their victims and the ripple effect of their actions. We would say to any victim, be open to the possibility of meeting your offender face to face. You don't have to shake their hand or care for them. It won't take the pain away nor is it a quick fix, but just hearing the words "I'm sorry" is a start to moving forward. For many of us, unless we face the person we have hurt and we see in their face what we have done we can't say 'sorry' and mean it. For us it was a life changing event.'

Speaking fondly about their son, Ray states: Chris was a fun, loving, hard working lad. He loved life and was a forgiving young man. Vi adds: "You have to choose to forgive and you have to choose to move on."

Source: Restorative Justice Council: http://www.restorativejustice.org.uk/ resource/ray_and_vi_donovan__meeting_our_sons_killer/

Seminar questions

1. What are the possible benefits of a restorative justice approach?
2. What are some of the limitations of the current criminal justice system when dealing with vulnerable witnesses and victims?
3. Restoration or retribution – which is a more appropriate aim?

Further reading

Christie, N. (1977) 'Conflicts as property', *The British Journal of Criminology,* **17, 1: 1–15**
This seminal article makes the argument that conflicts have been appropriated by the State through the criminal justice system, thereby sidelining the key parties involved.

Johnstone, G. (2002) *Restorative Justice: Ideas, Values and Debates.* **Cullompton: Willan Publishing**
This volume provides a very good introduction into the theories and practice of restorative justice.

Zehr, H. (1990) *Changing Lenses: A New Focus for Crime and Justice.* **Scottdale, PA: Herald Press**
Howard Zehr's work on restorative justice is one of the landmark texts in this area. This book presents a cogent rationale for a different approach towards justice.

Further information can be obtained from the following websites

Centre for Crime and Justice Studies: http://www.crimeandjustice.org.uk/
This is the website of an independent charity that advocates for a social justice approach towards the harms caused by crime. Its website contains a range of resources and provides links to current debates on some of the issues this chapter has raised.

International Institute for Restorative Practices: www.iirp.org
This website contains information on restorative practices worldwide and includes a wide range of learning resources on this topic.

Restorative Justice Council: http://www.restorativejustice.org.uk/
The Restorative Justice Council provides information about restorative justice in the UK. Usefully, this website also includes videos on the restorative justice process.

References

Ashworth, A. (2002) 'Responsibilities, rights and restorative justice', *British Journal of Criminology*, 42, 3: 578–96
Ashworth, A. & von Hirsch, A. (1998) 'Desert and the three "Rs"'. In: A. von Hirsch & A. Ashworth (eds) *Principled Sentencing: Readings on Theory and Policy*. Oxford: Hart Publishing
Becker, H.S. (1963) *Outsiders*. New York: The Free Press
Braithwaite, J. (1989) *Crime, Shame and Reintegration*. Cambridge: Cambridge University Press

Campbell, C., Devlin, R., O'Mahony, D., Doak, J., Jackson, J., Corrigan, T. & McEvoy, K. (2005) *Evaluation of the Northern Ireland Youth Conferencing Scheme*. Belfast: Northern Ireland Office

Christie, N. (1977) 'Conflicts as property', *British Journal of Criminology*, 17, 1: 1–15

Consedine, J. (1995) *Restorative Justice: Healing the Effects of Crime*. Lyttleton, New Zealand: Ploughshares Publications

Cory, G. (2011) *Summing Up: A Strategic Audit of the Criminal Justice System*. London: Victim Support

Daly, K. (2002) 'Restorative justice. The real story', *Punishment and Society*, 4, 1: 55–79

Davies, P., Francis, P. & Greer, C. (eds) (2007) *Victims, Crime and Society*. London: Sage

Dignan, J. (2007) 'The victim in restorative justice'. In: S. Walklate (ed.) *Handbook of Victims and Victimology*. Cullompton: Willan Publishing

Doherty, K. (2010) 'The development of restorative justice in Northern Ireland'. In: W. Taylor, R. Earle & R. Hester (eds) *Youth Justice Handbook: Theory, Policy and Practice*. Cullompton: Willan Publishing

Edwards, I. (2004) 'An ambiguous participant: The crime victim and criminal justice decision-making', *British Journal of Criminology*, 44, 6: 967–82

Erickson, K.T. (1962) 'Notes on the sociology of deviance', *Social Problems*, 9: 307–14

Eriksson, A. (2009) *Justice in Transition: Community Restorative Justice in Northern Ireland*. Cullompton: Willan Publishing

Hayes, D., Bunting, L., Lazenbatt, A., Carr, N. & Duffy, J. (2011) *The Experiences of Young Witnesses in Criminal Proceedings in Northern Ireland*. Belfast: NSPCC

Hirschi, T. (1969) *Causes of Delinquency*. Berkeley: University of California Press

Hoyle, C. & Zedner, L. (2007) 'Victims, victimization and criminal justice'. In: M. Maguire, R. Morgan & R. Reiner (eds) *The Oxford Handbook of Criminology*, 3rd edn. Oxford: Oxford University Press, pp. 461–95

Hoyle, C., Young, R. & Hill, R. (2002) *An Evaluation of the Implementation and Effectiveness of an Initiative on Restorative Cautioning*. York: Joseph Rowntree Foundation

Hudson, B. (2002) 'Restorative justice and gendered violence: Diversion or effective justice?', *British Journal of Criminology*, 42, 3: 616–34

Johnstone, G. (2002) *Restorative Justice: Ideas, Values and Debates*. Cullompton: Willan Publishing

Johnstone, G. (2003) *A Restorative Justice Reader: Text, Sources, Context*. Cullompton: Willan Publishing

Knox, C. (2001) 'The deserving victims of political violence: Punishment attacks in Northern Ireland', *Criminal Justice*, 1, 2: 181–201

Liebmann, M. (2007) *Restorative Justice: How it Works*. London: Jessica Kingsley Publishers

McAlister, S., Scraton, P. & Haydon, D. (2009) *Childhood in Transition: Experiencing Marginalization and Conflict in Northern Ireland*. Belfast: Queen's University, Prince's Trust Northern Ireland and Save the Children

McAra, L. & McVie, S. (2007) 'Youth justice?: The impact of system contact on patterns of desistance from offending', *European Journal of Criminology*, 4, 3: 315–45

McEvoy, K. & Mika, H. (2002) 'Restorative justice and the critique of informalism in Northern Ireland', *British Journal of Criminology*, 42, 3: 534–62

Maruna, S. (2011) 'Lessons for justice reinvestment from restorative justice and the justice model experience: Some tips for an 8-year-old prodigy', *Criminology & Public Policy*, 10, 3: 661–9

Maruna, S., Wright, S., Brown, J., van Merle, F., Devlin, R. and Liddle, M. (2007) *Youth Conferencing as Shame Management: Results of a long-term follow-up study*. Cambridge: ARCS (UK) Ltd

Morris, A. (2002) 'Critiquing the critics: A brief response to the critics of restorative justice', *British Journal of Criminology*, 43, 3: 596–615

Northern Ireland Office (2007) *Protocol for Community Based Restorative Justice Scheme*. Belfast: Northern Ireland Office

Restorative Justice Consortium (2004) *Principles of Restorative Justice Processes*. London: RJC. Available at: http://www.restorativejustice.org.uk/?Resources: Best_Practice:Principles

Shapland, J., Atkinson, A., Chapman, B., Colledge, E., Dignan, J., Howes, M., Johnstone, J., Robinson, G. & Sorsby, A. (2006) *Restorative Justice in Practice – Findings from the Second Phase of the Evaluation of Three Schemes*. London: Home Office

United Nations Office on Drugs and Crime (2006) *Handbook of Restorative Justice Programmes*. Vienna: United Nations

Zehr, H. (1990) *Changing Lenses: A New Focus for Crime and Justice*. Scottdale, PA: Herald Press

9 Conclusion

Beyond criminal justice?

Key issues

- Why have crime and justice become core areas of public debate?
- Why has there been an increased punitiveness in responses to crime?
- Is there scope for a more subtle picture to emerge?

Introduction

Criminal justice and our concepts or 'crime' and 'justice' are strongly influenced by social, cultural and political variables. The 'criminal justice system' comprises of an array of agencies with some distinct and overlapping purposes. As the opening chapter has identified, the rationale of the system can be more accurately described as an amalgamation of purposes – some complimentary and some contradictory. These concepts at any given time reflect the political and ideological position of the government on the issue of law, punishment and order.

This book began with a discussion about the meaning of crime and the role or roles of the criminal justice system. One of the key issues to note is that our understanding of crime is *socially constructed*. Rather than being viewed as a given, there are a variety of lenses through which crime can be viewed, for example, from a legalistic, sociological, political and/or psychological viewpoint. This is demonstrated by changes in definitions of what constitutes a criminal offence both over time and across different cultures.

One of the examples cited related to the decriminalisation of male homosexuality in the various jurisdictions of the UK. This example illustrates a number of themes, first of which is the manner in which the criminal justice system, oriented around a criminal code (i.e. law), is value-laden and linked to the maintenance of moral boundaries. Our response to and construction of crime are informed by cultural, temporal and spatial contexts. And the history of the decriminalisation of homosexuality, to take this one example, illustrates differences in laws and the administration of the criminal justice system in different parts of the UK, decriminalisation occurring at different stages in the various jurisdictions.

We have also noted variations in the age of criminal responsibility across the UK and the fact that the rates of imprisonment vary markedly, rising from a rate of 97 per 100,000 in Northern Ireland to 157 per 100,000 in England and Wales.[1] These differences are noteworthy in themselves, but especially if we view imprisonment as a measure of punitiveness; then the question has to be posed: why are there such differences? This can be explained in part by the differences in history, culture and structures of the systems.

Devolution and local contexts

We have argued that any analysis of the criminal justice system in the United Kingdom must take into account the fact that there are important differences in the criminal justice systems that operate in the different jurisdictions within the UK. While the English and Welsh systems are most similar, some analyses suggest that the Welsh system is becoming more distinct. Haines (2010), for example, has coined the phrase 'dragonization' to describe some of the distinguishing features between the Welsh and English youth justice systems. Although governed by the same legislation as England, distinctive youth justice organisational structures have been established in Wales, with a focus on implementing rights-based standards. Wales was also the first jurisdiction in the UK to appoint a Children's Commissioner (Haines, 2010; Muncie, 2011).

In Scotland and Northern Ireland there are significant differences in how the criminal justice system operates. The development of community-based restorative justice initiatives within Northern Ireland and the extent to which restorative justice has been embedded within the youth justice system is a notable example, as also is the traditionally welfarist orientation of Scotland's Children's Hearing System. These arise in different social, cultural, historical and political contexts. As Muncie (2011) notes, the devolution of power to local administrations adds another layer of complexity:

> The UK state now comprises a series of 'tangled territorial hierarchies' consisting of: the UK Parliament based in Westminster, London, a Parliament in Scotland, Assemblies in Northern Ireland and Wales, as well as Regional Development Agencies and an Assembly for London in England (Jones, 2001). Each of these has different powers and responsibilities. There is no common pattern. Nevertheless, the new constitutional arrangements have meant that some areas of policy making in the United Kingdom have been substantially regionalized and 'denationalized'. In particular, social policy reform, including youth justice reform, has become

a key element of the nation-building narratives that have come to prominence in a devolved United Kingdom. Constitutionally, however, the devolved institutions remain subordinate to the UK Parliament.

(Muncie, 2011: 41)

While the devolution of power to local assemblies may lead to further variation, it is worth noting that some of the most marked differences pertained before this power was devolved. Indeed, some commentators who observe that the localisation of criminal justice decision-making is no guarantee of a more benign system have voiced a note of caution. For example, Croall (2006), writing in the Scottish context, observes that there has been evidence of convergence of policies (notably in terms of increased punitiveness) elsewhere in the UK following Scottish devolution:

> It is perhaps ironic that a system that prided itself on being distinctive has seen greater convergence with England in the post-devolutionary era. . . . The introduction of widespread consultation and two Justice Committees has indeed drawn a wider range of actors into the process – not least politicians who have echoed the politicization of criminal justice, youth crime and antisocial behaviour south of the border and its 'popular punitivism' to a point where the control of antisocial behaviour is seen as a key policy area.
>
> (Croall, 2006: 602)

Croall's (2006) analysis points to the potential for increased politicisation of crime and justice issues in the context of local administrations. For example, after the devolution of policing and justice powers to the Northern Ireland Assembly in April 2010, following decades of political conflict, there have been debates about the need to increase public protection measures in relation to sexual offending (CJINI, 2010a). Controversial issues in Northern Ireland prisons such as the inadvertent release of prisoners have also been a cause of public debate accompanied by calls for the Justice Minister to resign (CJINI, 2010b; Owers *et al.*, 2011).

Culture(s) of control?

Muncie (2011) has more profoundly questioned whether there is merely the 'illusion of difference' in systems with administratively different structures but convergent concerns. This is evident in the common discourses of risk-oriented interventions and the emphasis placed on 'responsibilisation' of children and young people – that is, the individualisation of approaches that place the onus for change on the shoulders of individuals and which play down wider structural issues such as poverty and deprivation. As earlier chapters in this book have highlighted, these discourses are not unique to the youth justice system, but permeate across all parts of the criminal justice system in the United Kingdom, particularly in the sphere of prisons and probation.

Broad analyses of these trends consider that criminal justice policies and the responses of the criminal justice system have become increasingly characterised by punitiveness and managerial approaches (Bottoms, 1995; Feeley & Simon, 1994; Garland, 2001; O'Malley, 1982). Feeley and Simon (1994) coined the phrase 'new penology' to describe systems and process that have adopted actuarial approaches to the assessment, classification and management of crime and criminals. Symptomatic of this approach has been the over-arching emphasis placed on 'risk management'. In an analysis of the criminal justice system in America and the UK, Garland (2001) has argued that the ascendancy of the concept of risk and the collapse of welfarist approaches is characteristic of a 'culture of control'.

In his seminal text Garland (2001) identifies the following as the core indices of a 'culture of control':

- A changed tone in criminal justice policy;
- The re-emergence of punitive sanctions and 'expressive justice';
- The politicisation of law and order;
- A decline in the 'rehabilitative' ideal;
- The return of the 'victim';
- The expansion of crime prevention and community safety initiatives;
- A perpetual sense of crisis.

Bearing in mind the differences across the UK jurisdictions, Garland's (2001) typology provides a useful lens through which to look at the criminal justice system in the United Kingdom.

The tone of criminal justice policy and debate

The 'changed tone' of criminal justice policy has been seen in the manner in which 'law and order' has become a central plank of the government policy on crime. The rhetoric around discussions of crime often clouds more balanced debate. It has been shown that overall recorded crime levels have declined, and this has been a consistent pattern over a number of years. However, this fact would not be discernible from general discussions about crime. In the UK, both in the Westminster and Scottish parliaments and in the assemblies of Northern Ireland and Wales, the 'temperature' of debates on crime is constantly raised as various political parties fight to out-do each other on who can be 'toughest' in their response to crime. This *tone* can also be read across media and popular representations of crime and justice issues, and the sense in which crime is conveyed as a pervasive phenomenon affecting all of our lives.

The tone of debate and coverage on these areas, whether representative or not of realities, play an important role in structuring and shaping our perception of crime and criminality and in playing on our insecurities. Indeed, it has been argued that the illusion that the State can manage these insecurities while simultaneously, and paradoxically, playing a role in fashioning them, legitimises the role and authority of the State in this arena (Garland, 1996; Simon, 2007).

The politicisation of law and order

This has the effect of foreclosing debate about the purposes and functions of the criminal justice system. Consider the recent proposals of the Conservative Justice Secretary, Ken Clarke, to cut the length of sentences for offenders who plead guilty at the earliest opportunity. Part of the stated rationale for this proposal was to reduce the high numbers of people held in UK prisons, the population of which has risen exponentially since the 1980s. However, the Justice Secretary's proposals were scrapped because of fears that it would lead to accusations that the Tory party (traditionally conceived of as being a 'law and order' party) would be perceived to be 'soft on crime' – an apparently unforgivable electoral sin.[2]

The announcement that prisoners engaged in work should pay make payments towards victims of crime is another recent policy initiative that again echoes some of this punitive rhetoric. This can be seen in the Home Secretary's speech setting out his vision for the prison and criminal justice system in England and Wales (Box 9.1).

Box 9.1 Extract from Kenneth's Clarke Speech on 'Making prisoners pay to support victims'

Let's start with prisons. We need, in my opinion, to instill in our jails, a regime of hard work. Most prisoners lead a life of enforced, bored idleness, where even getting out of bed is optional. If we want to reduce the crimes these people will commit when they get out, we need as many as possible to get used to working hard for regular working hours. The ones prepared to make an effort need new opportunities to learn a trade. We have to try to get those with the backbone to go straight, to handle a life without crime when they have finished their punishment...

Do not worry. I have not become some woolly-minded idealist since I was last a reforming Minister. I am under no illusions about the British criminal class – I met plenty of them during my time at the Criminal Bar.

As well as a few since. I've never been in favour of mollycoddling criminals. Dangerous offenders must always, and will always be punished

---

with prison. But let us not deceive ourselves that the previous Government left 85,000 serious gangsters in prison, that our prisons are only populated by muggers, burglars and violent and dangerous individuals. We have 11,000 foreign prisoners in our jails. Our prisons contain thousands of anti-social petty criminals who fail to behave themselves in everyday life. Almost half are illiterate or innumerate. Almost half are mentally ill. The majority have a history of drug abuse. Sadly, far too many are former members of our armed services. Drifting along in lives of crime which their victims pay for over and over again. Too many go into prison without a serious drug problem and come out addicts. Ready, desperate, to commit more crimes to feed their habit. We have to do better than this.

Under New Labour, there weren't enough tough, demanding punishment options for judges. We have a real job on our hands to give judges those options. To improve punitive alternatives to prison. I do understand what the problem is with so-called Community Sentences. The public don't think they're tough enough. Judges and Magistrates aren't confident that they're tough enough. Well let me tell you that I have never thought that they were tough enough. The answer to that cannot be to give up. It must be to make community sentences as tough, respected and effective as they are in countries like France and Germany. When we consider how to reduce re-offending by rehabilitating released prisoners or providing tougher community sentences, I am interested in one thing – what works. Value for taxpayers money is best achieved by paying – not for good intentions – but for results.

Source: http://www.conservatives.com/News/Speeches/2010/10/Ken_Clarke_Making_prisoners_pay_to_support_victims.aspx

The tone of debate on crime and justice is linked to more punitive criminal justice responses. This is seen in the aforementioned rise in the prison population both in the adult and juvenile estates over the past thirty years. It is also seen in the expansion of the gaze of the criminal justice system beyond the realms of the prison. Chapter 5 on Probation and Community Justice notes that the numbers of people subject to community-based supervision has also risen markedly during this period. In 2009, the population under probation supervision was 241,500, representing an overall increase of 38 per cent in a ten-year period (MoJ, 2010). There is also a demonstrable *recycling effect* between the prison and probation populations, particularly with released prisoners who are returned to custody for breach of their licence conditions, a form of 'back-door' sentencing and re-entry route that has not been the subject of sufficient scrutiny (Padfield & Maruna, 2006; Weaver *et al.*, 2012).

Risk as a central organising principle

Alongside the increased numbers of people who are processed through the various agencies of the criminal justice system, the nature and experiences of the process has changed. This is most clearly evidenced in the manner in which *risk* has become a central governing principle of the criminal justice system. Policies and interventions are predicated and advanced on the basis that they are seen to be preventing or reducing risk. An increasing range of restrictive sanctions are justified on the basis that they are managing risk of 'future reoffending' and are therefore protecting the public from possible harm. The introduction of a range of *indeterminate* public protection sentences in various parts of the United Kingdom, where people are held in prison for unspecified lengths until their risk has been proven to be reduced, are evidence of this.

The assessment of risk in relation to future offending and risk of harm is built on a particular evidence base, described in the literature as the *risk factor prevention paradigm*. Some of the difficulties (or at least limitations) of this evidence base were set out in Chapter 7 on the Youth Justice system and responses to young people and crime. This includes the predictive validity of *risk factors* – in other words, the problems with prospectively predicting which people with these characteristics or experiences will become involved in offending (Haines & Case, 2008; Webster *et al.*, 2006). Furthermore, what are referred to as *risk factors* – such as poor school attendance, limited parental supervision or living in a high-crime area – are perhaps more appropriately interpreted as indicators of need (Gray, 2005).

Although there is a separate justice system for children and young people based on the understanding that these are a group with different needs, there is evidence of increased *adulteration* of the youth justice system (Muncie, 2008). This means a convergence of responses between the adult and youth justice systems – the emphasis on risk and public protection in both sectors is one example of this convergence.

Perhaps one of the most striking facts of the criminal justice system in the United Kingdom is the low age of criminal responsibility relative to other countries. As we discussed in Chapter 7, one of the key indicators of the perspective adopted in relation to young people and crime is the age at which children are deemed to be criminally responsible. In England, Wales and Northern Ireland the age of criminal responsibility is ten years. In Scotland the age of criminal responsibility is eight years, but under legislation passed in 2010, a child under the age of 12 years cannot be prosecuted for an offence.[3] Retaining such a low age of criminal responsibility is testament to the manner in which children and young people are viewed at the wider societal level, and to the fact that a criminal justice response becomes the mode through which services are delivered to children who elsewhere would be considered to be 'in need'.

Indeed, another key theme of the ascendancy of *risk* is the manner in which it has substituted *need* as a criterion for service delivery. This is evident in the term *criminogenic need*, which really refers to risks associated with reoffending. This emphasis illustrates the fact that the criminal justice system is not concerned with need or social inequality *per se*, rather with risks and how they can be managed. Thus the phrase *'resources follow risk'* has become axiomatic of the manner in which resources are allocated and services are delivered within the criminal justice system.

Decline of rehabilitation

In part this emphasis is related to the fact that previous incarnations or stated rationales for the criminal justice system, in particular for interventions with those who have been convicted of crime, have become discredited. Garland (2001) refers to this as the 'collapse of the rehabilitative ideal'. Here the question of *'what works?'* to reduce offending, as discussed in Chapter 5, has led to an increased emphasis on particular types of interventions such as *cognitive-behavioural* programmes, which target the 'thinking deficits' of individuals in an attempt to prevent further offending. While the evidence base for such approaches suggests *some* reductions in recidvism in *some* situations (Lipsey *et al.*, 2007), the utility of such approaches has also been critiqued (Mair, 2004; Ward & Maruna, 2007).

The earlier extract from Kenneth Clarke's speech also underlines that increased punitive functions are associated with community-based orders. Alongside the increased risk-focused nature of probation practice there has also been a hardening of the functions of probation. No longer an 'alternative to punishment' or an agency whose prime function is rehabilitation, probation is now firmly situated as an agency that delivers punishment.

The 'rise of the victim'

The increased attention paid to the victim of crime was noted in the previous chapter. Once considered marginal and almost incidental to the process, the victim has been afforded a renewed symbolic significance in the discourse of criminal justice. This is evident in a range of initiatives aimed at placing the victim 'at the heart of the criminal justice system'. The increased use of restorative justice approaches takes place in the context of dissatisfaction with the conventional retributive model of justice, where the victim continues to be marginalised. However, caution is voiced that restorative justice should not be considered a panacea. Some critics have argued that restorative justice approaches are inappropriate for particular types of crime, including domestic violence, sexual assault and hate crimes (Daly, 2002). Further, if restoration is the aim, the question for some is: restored to what?

A perpetual sense of crisis

A cursory view at newspapers or television screens on any given day will show how crime and criminal justice occupies a central space in everyday life. Reports of crime invariably lead to criticisms of system failures – police failing to act on information, prisoners being released in error, courts failing to convict a defendant etc. The overall result is the sense that crime is pervasive and that 'something should be done' to avert such crises. This leads to promises to 'do better'; in the political arena this manifests in political parties trying to out-do each other on who can be 'toughest' in response. This crisis state legitimises harsher sanctions and increased punitive measures.

In an analysis of criminal justice trends in the United Kingdom in the course of the twentieth century, Garland (1996) argues that an increased punitiveness is in fact a symptom of the limits of the State's control. Within these limits there are ranges of contradictory adaptations, strategies and responses. At the beginning of this book we argued that the criminal justice system is not a unitary system, rather it is an amalgamation of different rationales. This points to the need to consider points of divergence or differences across the criminal justice system.

A subtler picture?

This book critically analyses core issues in the criminal justice system in the United Kingdom. Several themes have been highlighted. It is also important in any analysis to look at points of difference. The fact that the United Kingdom is not a unitary entity in the administration of criminal justice has already been noted. Important also are significant differences *within* jurisdictions alongside differences *between* jurisdictions. Muncie (2011), for example, notes that Newcastle in the North of England has a lower proportion of young people sentenced to custody (2 per cent) than other parts of England, while one area in Wales (Merthyr Tydfil) has a custodial rate of 20 per cent.

This points to the need to look more closely at the *actual* implementation of policies and practices beyond the level of the broad brush-strokes described. Research that explores how practitioners within the system act on an individual level with clients provides some illumination of this theme (McNeill *et al.*, 2009). Cheliotis (2006), for example, has explored the manner in which practitioners within the criminal justice system have the capacity to subvert and resist punitive logic. Individual accounts of practice, such as Gregory's (2011) description of her career in probation, also speak to this theme.

Another important vein to note here is the role that participants have in shaping this process, for example, those who come into contact with the criminal justice system and are made subject to its sanctions. Different approaches to under-standing power speak to the role of resistance and agency on the part of subjects and the manner in which individuals shape, experience and influence processes (e.g. Foucault, 1978). This is not to ignore or underplay the range of structural issues that have been identified in this book, but rather to suggest a more subtle and potentially fruitful avenue of enquiry. In other words, there is a need to look at how those who are labelled offenders or victims also shape the system – sometimes through resistance.

Beyond criminal justice?

The critical lens applied to the criminal justice system in this book highlights that viewing problems as confined to questions of 'crime' or 'justice' has particular limitations. Wider questions of social harms such as inequality are overlooked in a criminal justice discourse (Hillyard *et al.*, 2004), and even on its own terms the criminal justice system fails to meet its aims, whether these are *public protection*, affording the victim a central role or managing risk. Looking beyond the parameters of criminal justice to make the links with wider social concerns is important. Exploring responses to the question of crime and criminality from the perspectives of *social justice* and human rights *are* possible lenses. Here the question is not just one of individual deficits but how wider environmental and structural influences affect individual lives.

There are some examples of approaches moving beyond an individualised deficit model. For example, the work on desistance within rehabilitation practice places an emphasis on building and strengthening social bonds. Chapter 6 discusses the use of imprisonment, and the concept of abolitionism is explored. This chapter questions the proliferation and the centrality of the use of imprisonment in society, and highlights the failures of prisons as either being reformative or able to reduce harm or control crime. The chapter goes on to argue that it is only by creating a new vision, a new language around crime, punishment and imprisonment grounded in a human rights and a social justice agenda, that traditional models of dealing with crime, penality and punishment can be challenged.

Conclusion

Understandings of crime and the response of the criminal justice system are shaped by social context. The increased attention paid to matters of crime and justice in media and public policy underlines the manner in which the discourse of crime (if not the direct experience of crime) shapes everyday life. Trends in criminal justice policy towards increased punitiveness have been influenced by public debate in this area and have manifested in increased numbers in custody and greater numbers of individuals being placed under the gaze of criminal justice agencies. This picture is not uniform, and there are variations in practice across and within jurisdictions.

Within the complex amalgam of rationales, different spaces, orientations and perspectives emerge, which ensure that criminal justice systems are situated on ever-shifting sands of policy and practice. However, within this context we argue that the ability of the criminal justice system to provide a 'just' response to all who come under its gaze raises profound questions about viewing social harms and ills through the prism of crime control.

Glossary

Culture of control – a term coined by Garland (2001) to refer to the social, economic and cultural factors that shape debates about crime and criminal justice responses.

Indeterminate sentence – these custodial sentences were introduced as part of public protection measures. The court will set a minimum tariff when sentencing, but the person will not be released until it has been satisfied that they no longer pose a serious risk to the public.

'New penology' – a term used by Feeley and Simon (1992) to describe the shift in emphasis in criminal justice from rehabilitation of the individual towards an aggregate approach to the assessment and management of risk.

Social justice – refers to approaches to society that are linked to equality and human rights.

Further reading

Bottoms, A., Rex, S. & Robinson, G. (eds) (2004) *Alternatives to Imprisonment: Options for an Insecure Society.* Cullompton: Willan Publishing
This edited collection contains chapters that critically explore the high imprisonment rates in the UK. Attention is paid throughout to alternatives to custody.

Garland, D. (2001) *The Culture of Control.* Oxford: Oxford University Press
David Garland's is a seminal book, which provides an overview and critical analysis of some key themes in criminal justice policy and practice in the Anglo-American context. He identifies a number of indices that he argues represent a *culture of control*, including the increased politicisation of criminal justice policy.

Simon, J. (2007) *Governing Through Crime: How the War on Crime Transformed American Democracy and Created a Culture of Fear.* Oxford: Oxford University Press
While the focus of Jonathan Simon's book is the increased punitiveness of the American criminal justice system, with an increasingly expansive prison population, the issues raised point to the politicisation of the crime and justice debate and have salience for the UK context.

References

Cheliotis, L. (2006) 'How iron is the cage of new penology? The role of human agency in the implementation of criminal justice policy', *Punishment and Society*, 8, 3: 313–40

CJINI (2010a) *An Inspection of the Handling of Sexual Offence Cases by the Justice System in Northern Ireland: Donagh Sexual Abuse Cases Inspection.* Belfast: Criminal Justice Inspection Northern Ireland

CJINI (2010b) *Northern Ireland Prison Service Mistaken Prisoner Releases.* Belfast: Criminal Justice Inspection Northern Ireland

Croall, H. (2006) 'Criminal justice in post-devolutionary Scotland', *Critical Social Policy*, 26, 3: 587–607

Daly, K. (2002) 'Restorative justice: The real story', *Punishment and Society*, 4, 1: 55–79

Feeley, M. & Simon, J. (1994) 'Actuarial justice: The emerging new criminal law'. In: D. Nelken (ed.) *The Futures of Criminology.* London: Sage, pp. 173–201

Foucault, M. (1978) (1991) 'Governmentality'. In: G. Burchell, C. Gordon & P. Miller (eds) *The Foucault Effect – Studies in Governmentality.* Chicago: University of Chicago Press, pp. 87–104

Garland, D. (1996) 'The limits of the sovereign state: Strategies of crime control in contemporary society', *British Journal of Criminology*, 36, 4: 445–70

Garland, D. (2001) *The Culture of Control.* Oxford: Oxford University Press

Goldson, B. & Muncie, J. (2006) 'Rethinking youth justice: Comparative analysis, international human rights and research evidence', *Youth Justice*, 6: 91–106

Gray, P. (2005) 'The politics of risk and young offenders' experiences of social exclusion and restorative justice', *British Journal of Criminology*, 45, 6: 938–57

Gregory, M. (2011) 'My probation career', *Probation Journal*, 58, 1: 37–51

Haines, K. (2010) 'Dragonization of youth justice'. In: W. Taylor, R. Earle & R. Hester (eds) *Youth Justice Handbook: Theory, Policy and Practice.* Cullompton: Willan Publishing

Haines, K. & Case, S. (2008) 'The rhetoric and reality of the "Risk Factor Prevention Paradigm" approach to preventing and reducing offending', *Youth Justice*, 8, 1: 5–20

Hillyard, P., Pantzis, C., Tombs, S. & Gordon, D. (eds) (2004) *Beyond Criminology: Taking Crime Seriously.* London: Pluto Press

Kilcommins, S., O'Donnell, I., O'Sullivan, E. & Vaughan, B. (2005) *Crime, Punishment and the Search for Order in Ireland.* Dublin: IPA

Lipsey, M.W., Landenberger, N.A. & Wilson, S.J. (2007) *Effects of Cognitive-Behavioural Programmes for Criminal Offenders.* Campbell Systematic Reviews, 6. DOI: 10.4073/csr.2007.6

McNeill, F., Burns, N., Halliday, S., Hutton, N. & Tata, C. (2009) 'Risk, responsibility, and reconfiguration', *Punishment & Society*, 11, 4: 419–42

Mair, G. (2004) *What Matters in Probation.* Cullompton: Willan Publishing

Ministry of Justice (2010) *Offender Management Caseload Statistics 2009. Ministry of Justice Statistics Bulletin.* London: Ministry of Justice

Muncie, J. (2008) 'The punitive turn in juvenile justice: Cultures of control and rights compliance in Western Europe and the USA', *Youth Justice: An International Journal*, 8, 2: 107–21

Muncie, J. (2011) 'Illusions of difference: Comparative youth justice in the devolved United Kingdom', *British Journal of Criminology*, 51, 1: 40–57

O'Malley, P. (1982) 'Risk, power and crime prevention', *Economy and Society*, 21, 3: 252–75

Owers, A., Leighton, P., McGrory, C., McNeill, F. & Wheatley, P. (2011) *Review of the Northern Ireland Prison Service.* Belfast: Prison Review Team

Padfield, N. & Maruna, S. (2006) 'The revolving door at the prison gate: Exploring the dramatic increase in recalls to prison', *Criminology and Criminal Justice*, 6, 3: 329–52

Priestley, P. & Vanstone, M. (eds) (2010) *Offenders or Citizens? Readings in Rehabilitation.* Cullompton: Willan Publishing

Prison Review Team (2011) *Review of the Northern Ireland Prison Service. Conditions, Management and Oversight of all Prisons. Interim Report.* Belfast: Prison Review Team

Simon, J. (2007) *Governing Through Crime: How the War on Crime Transformed American Democracy and Created a Culture of Fear.* Oxford: Oxford University Press

Ward, T. & Maruna, S. (2007) *Rehabilitation.* London: Routledge

Weaver, B., Tata, C., Munro, M. & Barry, M. (2012) 'The failure of recall to prison: Early release, front-door and back-door sentencing and the revolving prison door in Scotland', *European Journal of Probation*, 4, 1: 85–98

Webster, C., MacDonald, R. & Simpson, M. (2006) 'Predicting criminality? Risk factors, neighbourhood influence and desistance', *Youth Justice*, 6, 1: 7–22

Notes

1 What is crime?

1   *Criminal Justice (Scotland), 1980; Homosexual Offences (Northern Ireland) Order, 1982.*
2   Sutherland (1949: 9) defined a 'white collar crime' as 'a crime committed by a person of respectability and high social status in the course of his occupation'.
3   *Offences (Aggravation by Prejudice) (Scotland) Act, 2009.* The 2003 legislation, under *Section 74 of the Criminal Justice (Scotland) Act, 2003*, considers offences motivated by religious prejudice to be an aggravating factor.

2 What is the criminal justice system?

1   Similar legislation exists in Scotland and Northern Ireland.
2   The Home Office also retains responsibility for policing in England and Wales, while the Ministry for Justice in England and Wales has responsibility for prisons and probation.
3   The *Police and Criminal Evidence (Northern Ireland) Order, 1989* and attendant PACE codes are broadly similar in Northern Ireland.
4   Source data: *Criminal Justice Statistics Quarterly Update to September 2011. Ministry of Justice Statistics Bulletin*, p. 10; http://www.justice.gov.uk/downloads/ statistics/criminal-justice-stats/criminal-stats-quarterly-sept11.pdf
5   This data is from the International Centre for Prison Studies: http://www. prisonstudies.org/
6   *Criminal Justice and Licensing (Scotland) Act, 2010.*

3 Police and policing

1   On 13 July 2011, The Leveson Inquiry began its investigation into the role of the press and police in recent phone-hacking scandals.
2   Streamlining the police force has been a recent development. Prior to 1964, small municipal forces were in place (see Loader & Mulcahy, 2003).
3   Similar guidelines exist in Northern Ireland: *Police and Criminal Evidence (Northern Ireland) Order, 1989* and attendant PACE codes, but there is no Scottish equivalent.

4 Prosecution and the court process

1   The *Police and Criminal Evidence Act, 1984 (PACE) (England and Wales)* and *The Police and Criminal Evidence (Northern Ireland) Order, 1989 (Northern Ireland)* set out the law in this area.

2 The Code was most recently updated following the merger of the CPS with the Revenue and Customs Prosecutions Office (RCPO) in 2010. A similar code (issued in 2008) applies for the Public Prosecution Service in Northern Ireland. In Scotland, the rules pertaining to prosecution are set out in the *Crown Office and Procurator Fiscal Service Prosecution Code (2005)*.

3 Debbie Purdy was diagnosed with Multiple Sclerosis in 1985, and her condition has progressively worsened. She argued that it was a breach of her human rights not to know if her husband, Carlos Puente, would be charged with assisting her suicide if he took her to the Dignitas Clinic in Switzerland where she wishes to die (and where assisted suicide is legal) if her condition worsens. Debbie Purdy's case was eventually heard in the House of Lords in 2009, and led to the Lords ordering the Director of Public Prosecution to issue a policy statement to make clear if such cases were likely to be prosecuted: House of Lords Judgement: R (on the application of Purdy) (Appellant) *v* Director of Public Prosecutions (Respondent) [2009] UKHL 45.

4 In Glasgow some courts are presided over by a Stipendiary Magistrate (a legally qualified magistrate). The Stipendiary Magistrate's (SM) sentencing powers are greater than those of a Justice of the Peace. In a Justice of the Peace Court, a SM can impose a maximum sentence of 12 months' imprisonment or a fine not exceeding £10,000.

5 The last available report published in 2011 provides statistics on race and the criminal justice system for 2010. See Ministry of Justice (2011) *Statistics on Race and the Criminal Justice System 2010. A Ministry of Justice publication under Section 95 of the Criminal Justice Act 1991*. Available at: http://www.justice.gov.uk/downloads/statistics/mojstats/stats-race-cjs-2010.pdf

6 JUSTICE first called for an independent statutory body to investigate miscarriages of justice in 1964. It repeated this call in its 1989 report, *Miscarriages of Justice*, and when it gave evidence to the 1993 Royal Commission on Criminal Justice. The organisation's 1995 report, *Remedying Miscarriages of Justice*, set out a blueprint for the Criminal Cases Review Commission, which was established in 1997 as the CCRC.

5 Probation and community justice

1 A similar tool, the ACE (Assessment, Case Management and Evaluation Tool) is used by probation officers in Northern Ireland.

2 The availability of offending behaviour programmes in prisons has been a source of critical comment in numerous prison inspection reports.

3 *Probation Board (Northern Ireland) Order, 1982.*

6 Prisons and the abolitionist debate

1 Data on Northern Ireland Prison Service costs available from: http://www.ni prisonservice.gov.uk. Data on cost of imprisonment in England and Wales available from: NOMS (2011): 68.

7 Youth justice: Context, systems and practices

1 *Criminal Justice and Licensing (Scotland) Act, 2010.*

2 In 2010 the newly elected Conservative/Liberal Democrat coalition government announced plans for the abolition of the *Youth Justice Board*.

8 Restorative justice: An alternative mode?

1 ECOSOC Resolution 2002/12, *Basic Principles on the use of Restorative Justice Programmes in Criminal Matters.*
2 *Justice Northern Ireland Act, 2002.*
3 The crime and justice remit, which was part of the Northern Ireland Office, has since been superseded by the Northern Ireland Department of Justice, following the devolution of policing and justice powers to the Local Assembly in 2011.

9 Conclusion: Beyond criminal justice?

1 International Centre for Prison Studies: http://www.prisonstudies.org/.
2 'Kenneth Clarke denies another "U-turn" on sentencing', *The Guardian*, 21 June 2011.
3 *Criminal Justice and Licensing (Scotland) Act, 2010.*

Index